Every Child Reading

Darrell Morris

Appalachian State University

Robert E. Slavin

Johns Hopkins University

Boston   New York   San Francisco
Mexico City   Montreal   Toronto   London   Madrid   Munich   Paris
Hong Kong   Singapore   Tokyo   Cape Town   Sydney

Series Editor: *Aurora Martínez Ramos*
Editorial Assistant: *Beth Slater*
Senior Marketing Manager: *Elizabeth Fogarty*
Production Editor: *Kathy Smith*
Editorial-Production Service: *Chestnut Hill Enterprises, Inc.*
Composition Buyer: *Linda Cox*
Manufacturing Buyer: *JoAnne Sweeney*
Cover Administrator: *Kristina Mose-Libon*
Electronic Composition: *Galley Graphics, Ltd.*

For related titles and support materials, visit our online catalog at www.ablongman. com.

Between the time Website information is gathered and then published, it is not unusual for some sites to have closed. Also, the transcription of URLs can result in unintended typographical errors. The publisher would appreciate notification where these occur so that they may be corrected in subsequent editions.

Library of Congress Cataloging-in-Publication Data
    Morris, Darrell.
      Every child reading / Darrell Morris, Robert E. Slavin.
         p. cm.
      Includes bibliographical references and index.
      ISBN 0-321-08763-1
      1. Reading (Kindergarten) 2. Reading (Elementary) I. Slavin, Robert E. II. Title.
    LB1181.2 .M65 2003
    372.4—dc21

                                                                                        2002026046

Printed in the United States of America

10 9 8 7 6 5 4 3 2 1 VHG 07 06 05 04 03 02

Contents

Preface

Literacy is the key to academic success. However, schools have historically had difficulty teaching a sizeable minority of children to read. On entering the Information Age, our nation is concerned more than ever about getting all children off to a good start in reading. For example, many state legislatures have adopted higher standards for reading achievement in the primary grades. The federal government has also become involved. In 1997, Congress passed President Clinton's America Reads Challenge Act, which encouraged citizens to volunteer in the schools as reading tutors. Later, Congress appropriated new funds for reading program development and teacher training (Reading Excellence Act, 1998), and President Bush expanded this effort in his Reading First initiative (2002).

Still, there is much professional debate and controversy over how best to proceed in preventing reading failure. Do we opt for a new kind of beginning reading instruction, or try to modify and improve traditional practice? Do we heed the advice of practitioners who possess teaching experience, or follow the lead of researchers who possess empirical data? Finally, in seeking reform, do we invest our resources in materials and programs (as we have done in the past), or invest in improving the knowledge and skills of our teachers? Although these questions do not have to be stated in an either/or format, the choices actually reflect the history of our field and the professional battle lines that are being drawn today.

The present book is a collaboration between two reading professionals who do not agree on everything. Darrell Morris, of Appalachian State University in Boone, NC, is a teacher-educator who has developed reading tutoring models that are used throughout the country. Robert Slavin, of Johns Hopkins University, is a research psychologist who (along with Nancy Madden) developed Success for All, a comprehensive reading reform model for elementary schools that is used in forty-eight states. Because of our different training and experiences, we bring different perspectives to the issue of reforming beginning reading instruction. Morris, the clinical practitioner, is significantly influenced by the wisdom of practice (or craft) that has been handed down in reading education over the past one hundred years. Slavin, the researcher, is more influenced by empirical findings that clearly support specific teaching practices. Still, both of us share a belief that virtually every child can be a successful reader with good instruction and appropriate interventions, and both of us are pragmatists who believe that teachers should use what works, regardless of ideology or fashion. The fact that we agree on important goals but differ a bit on ways to pursue these goals should challenge the discerning reader of this book.

Every Child Reading is divided into five chapters. In a short opening chapter, Slavin defines the problem of early reading failure both in human and statistical terms. In Chapters 2 and 3, Morris offers a developmental perspective on teaching beginning readers in kindergarten and first grade. These chapters describe specific assessment, instructional, and management procedures that teachers can use in the classroom. In Chapter 4, Morris makes the case for one-to-one tutoring as the most effective intervention to prevent reading failure in the primary grades. Finally, in Chapter 5, Slavin provides an overview of Success for All, a comprehensive reform model for teaching reading in elementary schools. Many of the concepts introduced in Chapters 2 to 4 are reflected in Success for All; therefore, Chapter 5 serves as a model of *one* way to organize effective reading instruction in the primary grades.

The intended audience for this book includes preservice teachers, in-service teachers, and school administrators who are responsible for beginning reading instruction. We believe that each of these groups will benefit from the developmental, research-based perspective that the book provides.

The reading field has made important advances over the past three decades, both in knowledge of the reading acquisition process and in program development. Our challenge is to hold on to what we know to be sound theory and practice, while at the same time searching for new and more efficient ways to meet the needs of low readers. Teaching every child to read will eventually require *knowledge, problem solving,* and *will* on the part of individual teachers and the institutions within which they work. We dedicate this book to the educators who wrestle with this crucially important task every day.

We acknowledge the insightful observations of the following reviewers: Toni Bellon, North Georgia College and State University; Margaret L. Janz, Jackson University; Marsha Lewis, Kenansville Elementary School; Kathy Pike, Cambridge Central School District; Alice M. L. Quiocho, California State University, San Marcos; and Roxanne Reedyk, Riverview Alternative High School and Lakeland College.

1

Why Reading Reform Is Essential

Robert E. Slavin

Sara Esposito is frustrated. She's several months into the school year, and already she is concerned that many of her first graders aren't learning to read. Some of them haven't learned their letters or sounds. Some can sound out words but can't make sense out of the stories. Some appear to be able to read well and understand the books, but when they are given a new book they can hardly read a word. Some have trouble with English; it's doubly hard for them to be learning English and reading at the same time. Some probably could learn to read, but their behavior problems interfere with their ability to attend to reading. Some of Sara's children do read and comprehend well, but she has no idea why; she did pretty much the same things with these students as she did with the others, yet these children just seemed to have a knack for reading.

Sara has tried all kinds of things to improve her reading instruction. She attended a district in-service on "balanced literacy." She read articles in various teachers' magazines. She asked seasoned teachers in her school what to do. Sara has received lots of advice, but she doesn't know which to follow. Some ideas work with some of her children, while others don't seem to make much difference at all.

Sara's dilemma is a common one. Every year, she sees her children come into first grade bright-eyed, bushy-tailed, and eager to learn. She knows how smart, curious, and creative they are. Most of her children do learn to read, and she's proud of that. But year after year, too many children fail to read well enough. These children seem no less bright, no less highly motivated than the others, but something just doesn't click for them. Sara knows that while a few may be "late bloomers," most of her children who don't read well will never be good readers, which means that they may never be good students. Her children who don't read well are only dimly aware of this, but Sara looks at them with the eyes of experience and sees years of heartbreak, shame, and anger ahead. This is why she is so desperate to find a solution.

Sara's question is a straightforward one. She wants to know what she can do to ensure that every one of her children will learn to read. Everyone who reads this book, as well as the authors and the researchers who are cited, has the same question. What works? What can parents, teachers, principals, superintendents, board members, and legislators do to ensure that every child will be a confident, strategic, and capable reader?

Sara's dilemma is equally pressing if she has one child or thirty who are at risk for reading failure. It is equally pressing in middle-class schools and in high-poverty schools. The proportions of children who are struggling may be different in different schools, but it is a rare school that does not have at least a few students who are not reading adequately.

If reading failure were inevitable for a certain percentage of children, we might have a reason to be resigned to it, and do what we could to make the failure less painful. This is more or less what we've done for many years, putting ever-increasing numbers of students into special education and remedial programs that rarely, if ever, produce fully successful readers. However, research in recent years has begun to identify solutions to reading problems, especially means of preventing reading disabilities from developing in the first place. This research has not yet solved every problem of reading or literacy, far from it. But recent research is identifying effective, practical, and replicable means of ensuring the reading success of almost all children. Further, there are strategies that outstanding reading teachers have long used with success, and these time-tested and proven strategies could be beneficial for all teachers. We know more today than we did ten or twenty years ago, but more importantly we know much, much more today than is in widespread practice in schools. Research must continue, but if today's schools just used what today's research has already validated, the numbers of children failing in reading would be far less than what they are.

The purpose of this book is to present to today's educators and policymakers the best experience and evidence we have about how to answer Sara Esposito's simple question: "What works in reading?"

Is There a Reading Crisis?

Often, articles in the popular press and even in the education press make it appear that there was once a "golden age of reading," and that today's students are not learning to read as well as earlier students did. This is not true. The reading skills of America's children are not as good as they should be or could be, but they are not diminishing. The National Assessment of Educational Progress, affectionately known as NAEP, has been tracking reading achievement since 1971 (see Campbell, Hombo, & Mazzeo, 2000). Scores for nine-year-olds (the youngest students tested) have remained virtually unchanged for the entire time (see Figure 1.1). In fact, there

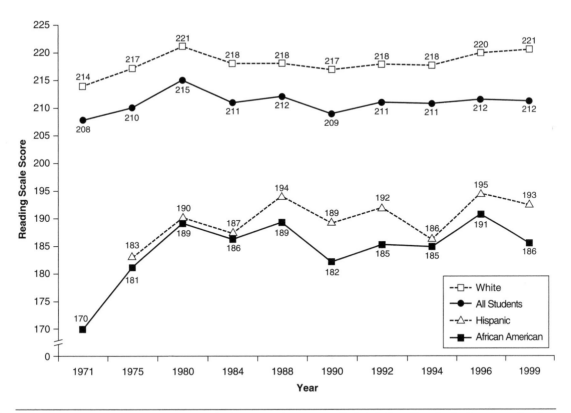

FIGURE 1.1 *National Assessment of Educational Progress (NAEP), Reading Scale Scores at Age 9 by Ethnicity, 1971–1999*

Data are from Campbell et al., 2000.

is one very important aspect in which things have gotten better. During the 1970s and 1980s, the gap between Caucasian students and African American and Latino students diminished. Also, an international study of reading found that U.S. fourth graders were among the best in the world in reading, significantly behind only Finland.

The problem in reading is not that reading performance is dropping, but that it is not increasing. In what other area of American life would we be satisfied to say that things have gotten no worse since 1971? Most importantly, there are far too many children who have extremely poor reading skills, and these children remain disproportionately poor and minority. On the 1998 NAEP, 27 percent of Caucasian students scored below the "basic" level. This is hardly cause for celebration; "basic" is a very minimal requirement, and to have 27 percent of students below this is unacceptable. However, the results were far, far worse for minority students. Sixty-four percent of African American students, 60 percent of Hispanic students, and 53 percent of American Indian fourth graders scored below "basic." Asian/ Pacific Islander students also performed less well than Caucasians, at 31 percent below basic.

By twelfth grade, 17 percent of Caucasian students, 43 percent of African American students, 36 percent of Hispanics, 35 percent of Indians, and 25 percent of Asian/Pacific Islanders were below the basic level. The primary reason for these gaps is the impact of poverty. Among other things, disadvantaged children in the United States have both fewer family resources to support literacy (such as books in their home) and are far more likely to attend underfunded, inadequate schools than are children from more affluent homes. Whatever the reasons, however, this level of reading failure is utterly unacceptable. A student who leaves school reading at such a low level is unemployable in any but the most menial occupations. It's easy to see how many of our most fundamental societal problems would be alleviated if every student could read adequately. More importantly, the damage done to individual children who cannot read well is profound. This is why Sara Esposito is so determined to find a solution to the reading problems of her first graders. She's not thinking so much about racial inequities or building a knowledge-based economy or making America first in the world in reading. She's thinking about individual children, full of hope, who could end up living their whole lives without books, without newspapers, without a love of learning, and without positive self-esteem based on success in school.

The purpose of this book is to present effective reading strategies, based on the best research we know about as well as our own experiences and those of the thousands of teachers we've worked with over the years. It is not our purpose to try to review every study or theory anyone has ever done; there are other sources for detailed reviews of the literature (see, for example, National Reading Panel, 2000; Snow, Burns, & Griffin, 1998). What we are trying to do instead is to distill the findings of research and experience and make them accessible to the people who really matter in the education of young children: teachers, principals, and other educators whose dedication, skill, and knowledge will make all the difference in the reading performance of today's students.

Every Child Reading: What Would It Take?

What would it take to ensure that every child in the United States became a capable, confident, and joyful reader? First, it is important to acknowledge that there is no single solution that would reach every child. For example, children who have learning difficulties have different needs from those who find reading easy; children whose home language is not English have different needs from those who speak standard English.

We might propose the following rough categories of young readers (see Slavin, 1998):

Natural Readers (40–50% of children). There is a large group of children who seem to learn to read no matter what. Often, these are children who were read to from an early age, whose parents clearly value reading and read frequently themselves, who developed excellent language skills, knowledge of how the world works, and knowledge about sounds and letters before their first day in school. However, even children without all of these advantages are often natural readers, and learn to read with little apparent effort regardless of teaching method. These children still need good teaching to achieve their full potential as readers and writers, but will never be in danger of reading failure.

Natural readers often give teachers (and researchers!) a false sense of efficacy, and they help explain why so many reading fads can sustain themselves for some period of time; natural readers will make any teacher and any teaching method look marvelously effective.

Teachable Readers (30–40% of children). Another group of chliciren we might distinguish are those who can learn to read with effective instruction, but who would be at risk without it. For these children, the quality of reading instruction they receive, especially in the early grades, can literally be the difference between success and failure throughout their schooling and, therefore, throughout their lives. Unlike a natural reader, a teachable reader is likely to need a well-organized, step-by-step approach to reading instruction, frequent assessment, and immediate intervention if things start to go wrong. Yet with such instruction, teachable readers are likely to be able and motivated readers and fully successful students. Of the 38 percent of all fourth graders who score below the "basic" level on NAEP, we believe that the great majority are children who could have learned to read well with the right classroom instruction and support but did not receive instruction appropriate to their needs.

Tutorable Readers (10–20% of children). Tutorable readers are those who are at risk for reading failure even with good-quality classroom instruction, but who could be adequate readers if they have well-structured tutoring in the early grades. Many of these children can succeed with well-trained volunteers or paraprofessionals (see Morris, 2001; Wasik, 1997), but some need more highly-trained tutors who are likely to have teaching certificates and specialized training (Wasik & Slavin, 1993).

Additional categories of potential readers who need individual attention (in addition to good teaching) include children who need eyeglasses, hearing aids, behavioral or emotional interventions, family services, or other nonacademic assistance to be able to profit from classroom instruction and (if necessary) tutoring.

Tutorable children constitute a very large proportion of children who are unnecessarily assigned to special education for reading disabilities, who are by definition children of normal intelligence who nevertheless failed to learn to read. There is a great deal of evidence that from half to two thirds of children categorized as learning disabled could have learned to read with some combination of tutoring and high-quality classroom instruction (see Lyons, 1989; Silver & Hagin, 1990; Slavin, 1996).

True Dyslexics (1–2% of children). A very small proportion of children would not learn to read even with high-quality classroom instruction and one-to-one tutoring. This is surely a far smaller group than the number currently assigned to special education for learning disabilities (about 5% nationally), because it excludes those who would have learned to read with tutors. Children in this category may benefit from more intensive and multisensory therapies.

English Language Learners. Children who do not speak English at home may fall into any of the above categories, but their limited proficiency in English adds an additional problem. It is unclear whether bilingual (native-language) or English immersion is best for these children, but what is clear is that the quality of instruction for English language learners is extremely important (see August & Hakuta, 1997; Slavin & Calderón, 2001). If children are taught in their native language, they must learn to read well in that language and then experience effective programs to help them make the transition to English reading. If they are taught in English, they need accommodations in their classroom instruction as well as assistance to help them rapidly acquire the English spoken in school.

A comprehensive strategy designed to ensure the success of all students must take all of these categories into account. It must provide research-based, effective instruction to all children, tutoring or other services for those who need it, and appropriate instruction for English-language learners. We cannot reduce the percentage of inadequate fourth grade readers from 38 percent (the proportion below basic on NAEP) to zero overnight, and maybe we'll never make it all the way to that goal. However, there is no reason that all teachable and tutorable children cannot be successful readers, while we learn to chip away at the last, very small proportion of children we cannot reach with today's methods.

The point of this discussion is to illustrate how one-shot, simple-minded solutions won't ensure success for every child. By themselves, standards won't do it, phonics won't do it, tutoring won't do it, new therapies for dyslexia won't do it, strategies for English-language learners won't do it, parental involvement won't do it. But all of these together, with the staff, resources, and professional development needed to ensure quality and effectiveness, can bring us to a day when reading failure is extremely rare. Some of the problems of education may be intractable, but reading for all is not one of them. This is a problem we can solve.

References

August, D., & Hakuta, K. (1997). *Improving schooling for language-minority children: A research agenda.* Washington, DC: National Research Council.

Campbell, J. R., Hombo, C. M., & Mazzeo, J. (2000). *Trends in academic progress: Three decades of student performance.* Washington, DC: U.S. Department of Education.

Morris, D. (2001). The Howard Street tutoring model: Using volunteer tutors to prevent reading failure in the primary grades. In L. Morrow & D. Woo (Eds.), *Tutoring programs for struggling readers: The America Reads challenge* (pp. 177–192). New York: Guilford.

Lyons, C. A. (1989). Reading Recovery: A preventative for mislabeling young "at risk" learners. *Urban Education, 24,* 125–139.

National Reading Panel. (2000). *Teaching children to read: An evidence-based assessment of the scientific research literature on reading and its implications for reading instruction.* Rockville, MD: National Institute of Child Health and Human Development.

Silver, A. A., & Hagin, R. A. (1990). *Disorders of learning in childhood.* New York: Wiley.

Slavin, R. E. (1996). Neverstreaming: Preventing learning disabilities. *Educational Leadership, 53*(5), 4–7.

Slavin, R. E. (1998). Far and wide: Developing and disseminating research-based programs. *American Educator, 22*(3), 8–11, 45.

Slavin, R. E., & Calderón, M. (Eds.). (2001). *Effective programs for Latino students.* Mahwah, NJ: Erlbaum.

Snow, C. E., Burns, S. M., & Griffin, P. (Eds.). (1998). *Preventing reading difficulties in young children.* Washington, DC: National Academy Press.

Wasik, B. A. (1997). Volunteer tutoring programs: Do we know what works? *Phi Delta Kappan, 79*(4), 282–287.

Wasik, B. A., & Slavin, R. E. (1993). Preventing early reading failure with one-to-one tutoring: A review of five programs. *Reading Research Quarterly, 28,* 178–200.

2

Reading Instruction in Kindergarten

Darrell Morris

Kindergarten is the critical year in which young children make the transition from the home or preschool to the elementary school. It is a year for social learning—learning to share, to take turns, and to wait patiently for an adult's attention. It is a year for oral language development and exploration with art and music. And, it is a year for academic preparation—learning about the community, learning basic math and science concepts, and learning the rudiments of literacy.

More than any other group of educators, kindergarten teachers are concerned about the *developmental appropriateness* of learning activities. They fully appreciate the intellectual enthusiasm and curiosity of their five-year-old charges and in no way wish to stifle this vital urge to learn with a curriculum that is either too challenging or lacking in interest. With regard to reading instruction, the kindergarten teacher faces two major challenges: (1) to provide children with engaging, doable, reading-related tasks; and (2) to choose a curriculum or set of tasks that prepares children for success in a first-grade reading program. In light of the enormous diversity among five-year-olds in home and preschool experiences, cognitive and emotional development, and other factors, balancing these two challenges is a formidable task. Nonetheless, both must be be met if a kindergarten reading program is to be developmentally appropriate (McGill-Franzen, 1992).

A true story, a cautionary tale, calls attention to the kindergarten teacher's responsibility for reading instruction. Several years ago, while screening at-risk first-grade readers nominated by their teachers for possible inclusion in a tutorial program, I happened to be working in two schools within the same rural county. In the first school, which served a middle-class population, in September the children could name at least twenty letters of the alphabet, knew most of the consonant letter–sound relationships, and could match spoken words to printed words as they echo-read short texts. In the second school, which served a poor to working-class population, the children could, on average, name only ten alphabet letters, knew few letter–sound relationships, and had no idea how spoken words matched to printed words in the act of reading. Because I understood the importance of alphabet knowledge and print awareness in the early stages of learning to read, I knew that the first graders in the middle-class school had a decided advantage over the first graders in the working-class school. In a one hundred-yard race, the former were starting off with a twenty-yard lead.

I mentioned the "reading readiness" difference to the county's language arts coordinator and surmised that the two schools must have very different kindergarten preparation programs. To my surprise, she stated that there was actually little kindergarten reading instruction going on in either school; in fact, most kindergarten teachers in the county had adopted a "hands-off" approach to reading, deeming it inappropriate to teach five-year-olds formal reading skills. If a difference in kindergarten instruction was not the answer, then why were the entering first graders in the two schools so different in alphabet and print-related knowledge? Obviously, the children in the middle-class school, in comparison to those in the working-class school, had received more reading and writing experiences *in the home*, and thus were bringing more knowledge with them to first grade. In a sense, the school district's kindergarten program was not fulfilling its traditional role of "leveling the playing field"; it was not preparing the children most in need of help (i.e., those with little prior literacy experience) for the reading challenges they would face in first grade.

This is not to say that the kindergarten teachers in the above situation were not providing important instruction. Most likely these teachers were developing their students' experiential knowledge and oral language through a variety of meaningful and enjoyable activities. Nonetheless, the teachers were overlooking print-related instruction (letters, sounds, words) that is fundamental to success in a first-grade reading program. In this chapter I will argue that such print-related understandings need to be taught in the kindergarten year, and that they can be taught in a developmentally appropriate manner within the context of an engaging and meaningful curriculum.

A Kindergarten Reading Program

The kindergarten reading program described in this section includes four core activities: reading aloud to children, guided contextual reading, letter–sound study, and writing. These literacy activities are meant to extend and support, not supplant, a meaningful, experience-based curriculum of science, art, math, and social studies.

Reading Aloud to Children

Educators have long known that young children who are read to extensively in the pre-school years tend to get off to a good start in first-grade reading (Bus, van Ijzendoorn, & Pelligrini, 1995). But why is this so? In his book, *The Meaning Makers*,

Gordon Wells (1986) pointed out some obvious advantages of reading aloud to children. Such storybook (or content book) reading helps children extend their experiences beyond their immediate surroundings, provides them with a vocabulary to name the new experiences, and acquaints them with the characteristic rhythms and structures of written language (which are different from those of spoken language).

Wells went on to identify two other not-so-well-known advantages of reading stories aloud to children. Contrasting picture-naming in a magazine with listening to a story, he stated:

> Listening to a story read aloud, on the other hand, provides a different sort of introduction to written language. Here what is encountered is continuous prose, in which meaning is built up cumulatively over many sentences and even chapters (p. 150).

In other words, listening to a story involves the child in creating a mental image and sustaining it over time (over several pages) in a quest for meaning. Such sustained mental-image building (using written language as the input) is not usually found in picture naming or in the here-and-now exchanges of casual adult–child conversation.

In describing a final and, to his mind, crucially important role for story reading, Wells drew a distinction between written language and spoken language. He noted that, in a spoken interchange, there is a shared context, and the listener can draw on features of this context (e.g., the kitchen, front yard, playground), along with the speaker's gestures and intonation, to interpret the speaker's meaning. The aim in conversational speech, stated Wells (1986, p. 156), is "to make the words fit the world." In most writing, however, there is no external context (no shared setting, gestures, or intonation) to help communicate meaning between author and reader. In this case, the writer must, in Wells's terms, "use words to create a world of meaning." And the reader's (or, in our case, listener's) task is to reconstruct this world by interpreting the author's words. Wells stated:

> To understand a story therefore—or any other written text—the child has to learn to give full attention to the linguistic message in order to build up a structure of meaning. For, insofar as the writer is able to provide cues for the reader's act of construction, he or she does so by means of the words and structures of the text alone.
>
> What is so important about listening to stories, then, is that, through this experience, the child is beginning to discover the symbolic potential of language: its power to create possible or imaginary worlds through words—by representing experience in symbols that are independent of the objects, events, and relationships symbolized (p. 156).

Reading to children, then, allows them to exploit the symbolic potential of language—to use language symbols to create a mental world beyond the present context. This, to Wells, and to others (see Donaldson, 1978) is the ultimate advantage of reading stories to children. It helps to make them literate.

From ages two to five, many children are read to in the home on a consistent basis. On entering school, these fortunate ones, for the reasons mentioned above, are already set up for reading—tuned in and ready to go (see Holdaway, 1979; Snow, Burns, & Griffin, 1998). For those less fortunate children who have not been read to extensively during the preschool years, the kindergarten year provides a crucial learning opportunity. These children must be read to on a daily basis if they are to catch up with their peers, to develop what Holdaway termed a "set for literacy." Wells (1986) even went so far as to recommend that volunteers be brought into kindergarten and first-grade classrooms to read storybooks to children on a one-to-one basis.

One-to-one reading-to experiences may not be necessary, however. A good story, pictures and all, can easily be shared with a group of twenty kindergarteners nestled in a corner of the classroom. As the teacher reads aloud, he or she will want to stop the story now and then to define a new word, to discuss a character's motives, or to have the children predict what might happen next in the plot. However, "the story's the thing," and through the teacher's daily reading aloud of good material, the children will gradually internalize the structure, cadence, and meaning-bearing characteristics of written language.

Interestingly, reading aloud to kindergarteners prepares them not just for first grade, but also for the literacy demands of later grades. Whereas first-grade reading texts are necessarily simplified to help children master the mechanics of reading, second- and third-grade texts are more complex in terms of vocabulary, syntax, and comprehensibility. It stands to reason that reading aloud to children in kindergarten can prepare them for the increasingly complex written language they themselves must learn to read as they advance through the primary grades.

While reading stories aloud to children is of great importance, there is a need for another type of kindergarten reading instruction; that is, print-related instruction (e.g., concepts of print, alphabet, letter–sound correspondences, early sight vocabulary) that prepares children for the unique demands of first-grade reading. It is to this topic that I now turn.

Contextual Reading

Teaching children to read can be approached in several ways. One can start by teaching them to blend individual letter–sounds (*c-a-p = cap*); to memorize individual words (e.g., *boy, girl, cat, and, the*); or to echo-read (teacher reads, then child echos) simple texts. Although the first two approaches will not be ignored, I begin with *echo reading of simple texts,* an approach that affords young children a concrete, supportive, and meaningful entry into reading. There are two major methods or contexts associated with echo reading: (1) dictated experience stories, and (2) big books (enlarged books with predictable text). These will be discussed separately and then some similarities and differences between the two methods will be noted.

Dictated Experience Stories. The method of dictated experience stories, sometimes referred to as the language-experience approach, has been used to teach children to read for over one hundred years (see Huey, 1908; Stauffer, 1970; Templeton, 1997). The method involves using children's own experiences, recorded in their own language, to teach them to read. That is, a shared experience is recounted or dictated by a group of children, written down on chart paper by the teacher, and then read and reread by the children with the teacher's support.

There is no one best way to conduct a dictated experience story lesson. Any approach that has been around for one hundred years will have been adapted in different ways by those practitioners who have used it. What follows is one suggested three-day cycle for reading a single experience story with a class of kindergarteners.

Day 1. The teacher leads the children in a discussion of a shared experience, for example, making popcorn, making valentine cards, watching snowflakes fall, visiting the school library or cafeteria, planting a seed, retelling the story of Columbus's voyage, and so on. Following three to five minutes of oral discussion, the children dictate two or three sentences describing the experience, and the teacher records these few sentences in manuscript print on a large sheet of chart paper.

> *Making Popcorn*
> We made popcorn.
> We made it in a popcorn popper.
> We put butter and salt on the popcorn.

Next, the teacher models a reading of the completed story, pointing to each word as he/she reads. Finally, the children join in choral reading the story several times, with the teacher continuing to point to the words on the chart paper as the group reads.

Day 2. The Day 1 "Popcorn" story is brought out and choral-read several times, with the teacher again modeling finger-point reading. Next, the teacher asks some questions regarding the now familiar three lines of print. For example:

- Who can come up to the chart and show me where we start reading? Where we end? Where do we go when we reach the end of a line?
- These little dots in our story are called 'periods.' What do they tell us to do?
- Who knows this word [teacher points to *popcorn*]? Good! Can someone else find the same word at another place in the story?
- What is the first letter in this word [teacher points to the *p* in *put*]? Can you find another word in our story that begins with a *p*?

Day 3. On Day 3, the teacher works at a table with groups of six to eight children at a time. The "Popcorn" story has been transferred from the large chart paper to the bottom half of an 8" by 11" sheet of paper, and each child at the table has a copy. The teacher reads the story several times and the children attempt to follow along on their own copy. Next, the teacher instructs the children to illustrate the "Popcorn" story on the top half of their paper. As the children begin to draw, the teacher moves around to each child and asks him or her to finger-point read the three-line story. (Early in the year, the teacher may have to use an echo-reading strategy. That is, the teacher reads one or two lines, then the child attempts to finger-point read the same lines.) If the child is successful in finger-point reading the story—that is, matching spoken words to written words in an appropriate manner—the teacher can afterward point randomly to individual words in the text and see if the child can identify them, either immediately or by using context.

Kindergarten children will differ considerably in their ability to finger-point read a short, familiar text like "Making Popcorn." Therefore, the Day 3 procedure described above, aside from its instructional value, is important diagnostically. It allows the teacher to observe carefully the reading development of individual children at a low cost in time, 1 minute spent with each child.

In kindergarten, one or two new dictated stories can be introduced each week and, on occasion, "old" favorites brought out and reread. Below is a possible weekly schedule:

Monday:	Create and read dictation #1
Tuesday:	Reread dictation #1; explore dictated story for specific words and letter–sounds
Wednesday:	Illustrate dictation # 1; teacher observes individual children reading dictation #1
Thursday:	Create and read dictation #2; teacher finishes observations on dictation #1
Friday:	Reread dictation #2; explore dictated story for specific words and letter–sounds

An important factor for the teacher to keep in mind is the length of story. In October, kindergarteners may enjoy dictating seven or more sentences about a Halloween experience, but the resulting printed story will be too long and complicated for them to read. The teacher needs to control story length so that, at a given point in the year, the children can memorize the text and successfully practice finger-point reading and word and letter location. For example, two to three sentences will suffice during the first month of school. This could be raised to four sentences by mid year, and to five or six sentences by the end of the year.

Big Books. The "big book" or shared book-experience method (Holdaway, 1979; Routman, 1988) is a fairly recent approach to teaching beginning reading. Imported from New Zealand to the United States in the mid-1980s, the big book method is theoretically sound and highly motivating. For good reason, it has now become a teaching staple in American kindergarten and first-grade classrooms.

The big books themselves have two defining characteristics: (1) The pictures and accompanying print are oversized (page size is approximately 18" × 24") so that a large group of children sitting around a teacher can follow along visually as the teacher reads; and (2) the language patterns in most big books are natural and rhythmic, oftentimes featuring repetitive refrains. As one can see in *Mrs. Wishy-Washy* (Cowley, 1980; Figure 2.1), there is much repetition of reading vocabulary built into big books. In this 102-word book, the high-frequency words, *mud, said, she, in, it, the,* and *went,* are each repeated four or more times. Furthermore, the repetition

FIGURE 2.1 *Example of predictable text found in the big book,* **Mrs. Wishy-Washy.** *(© Wright Group/McGraw-Hill).*

of sight words—very important to a beginning reader—occurs in a predictable context of natural-sounding sentence patterns. As one teacher put it, "After a few pages, the book almost reads itself."

For the teacher, guiding the reading of a big book is much like guiding the reading of a dictated story. On Day 1, the teacher introduces a new book by reading it aloud to the children and asking them questions about the story line. A wooden pointer is used to track the individual words as they are read. Next, the children join the teacher in a second reading of the story. On Day 2, the class choral-reads the same story one or more times, with the teacher again modeling how to point to each word. As a follow-up activity, the teacher may have individual children come up and finger-point read a given page or identify specific words on the page. Or the teacher may demonstrate how to use sentence context, picture cues, and a beginning letter-sound to help identify an unknown word in the text (e.g., "Oh lovely mud," said the pig, and he r_____ in it .). On Day 3, the teacher works with small groups, observing individual children's ability to finger-point read small sections of the story.

As with dictated stories, the length of a big book, and especially the amount of text on each page, are important considerations. Kindergarteners, particularly at the beginning of the year, benefit from reading big books containing only one or two lines of text per page. It is in this simplified context that the children have the best chance of figuring out directionality of print, the spoken word–written word match, and the role of beginning consonant cues in word recognition.

Small copies of big books (and typed copies of dictated stories) can be sent home for additional practice with parents or other family members. This helps to build home–school literacy connections, allows students to "show off" their learning, and underscores reading as a lifetime activity rather than only a school task.

Similarities and Differences between Dictated Stories and Big Books. There are several similarities and two major differences between the two reading methods discussed thus far. The similarities are:

- Both dictated stories and big books feature natural language patterns as opposed to the stilted, formulaic language found in most basal preprimers.
- In both methods, the reading process is continually modeled by the teacher via her finger-point reading of the text. Young children benefit from models they can imitate when they are trying to master a complex task like reading.
- Both methods emphasize group choral reading of stories, which helps to minimize the threatening aspect of learning to read. Individuals feel protected and supported by the group as they make their first, tenuous attempts at reading text.
- Both methods rely on memory and repetition to support children's initial reading attempts. Children are encouraged to memorize a dictated story or big book through repeated readings. With the memory of a specific story lodged in their heads, they can begin to explore how that story (or text) is represented in lines of print (i.e., which spoken lines match to which printed lines; which spoken words match to which printed words).

- Finally, both the dictated story and big book methods provide a rich, multi-layered language experience that individual children can draw from at different levels. For example, as the teacher models a finger-point reading of a big book, one child in the group may actually be learning sight words; another child may be figuring out how the spoken words match to printed words; and still another, though oblivious to the teacher's pointing, may be enjoying and internalizing the cadence of the book language.

Similarities notwithstanding, there are two significant differences between the dictated story and big book methods:

- The language patterns found in dictated stories and big books are different. Dictations, by definition, contain the *spoken* sentence patterns of kindergarten-aged children; big books contain the *written* sentence patterns of children's literature.
- Dictated stories allow kindergarteners to capture and preserve shared classroom experiences by writing them down in their own language. Big books, on the other hand, present new literary experiences to children (settings, story plots, and vocabulary terms).

Because of both their underlying similarities and distinctive differences, dictated stories and big books complement each other nicely in a beginning reading program. In fact, the consistent use of both methods in the kindergarten classroom will extend children's experiences and nurture their language development (particularly important for second-language learners), and also help them master some basic print-related understandings. For example, over time the kindergarteners will learn to read left to right, to match spoken words to printed words as they read, and to use sentence context along with beginning consonant cues to identify words in text. They may even commit a few sight words to memory. Such is the power of teacher-guided echo reading in simple but interesting stories.

Alphabet, Phoneme Awareness, and Letter–Sound Correspondences

While guided reading of stories provides the "whole" or the meaningful frame for reading acquisition, there are also important "bits" to be learned. Among these bits are the alphabet, phoneme awareness, and letter–sound correspondences. *Alphabet knowledge* is the ability to name and write the twenty-six alphabet letters; *phoneme awareness* is the ability to attend to the individual sounds within a spoken word (e.g., the /b/, /ă/, and /t/ sounds in *bat*); and *letter–sound knowledge* is just what it says: knowledge of the conventional letter–sound pairings in written English (e.g., *b* – /b/; *r* – /r/; *a* – /ă/; etc.). Although the three can be considered separately, in the teaching of beginning reading they are often intertwined.

The alphabet letters are the building blocks of our writing system and an important knowledge source for beginning readers (Ehri & Wilce, 1985; Stahl &

Murray, 1994). A given alphabet letter (e.g., *B*, b) and the sound that it represents (/b/) are usually taught together. There is no one best way to do this. Some kindergarten teachers use a thematic approach to introduce one or two letter-sounds a week. For example, if the class is studying the letter *b*, the teacher might begin by writing the letter *B–b* on the chalkboard and providing its name ("bee") and sound (/b/). Then, for the next few days, the children not only practice writing the letter *b*, but also proceed to draw "b" pictures ("ball," "bird," "bike," etc.), search for "b" items in magazines, and bring in "b" objects from home. Other teachers may use more common but equally effective tasks to teach letter-sounds, including phonics workbooks, pencil-and-paper copying, and cut-and-paste activities.

Of one thing the teacher of alphabet letters and letter–sound correspondences can be sure: the need for review. As individual letter-sounds are introduced over the course of a few weeks, some children will retain what they have been taught, others will not. The kindergarten teacher must be vigilant, assessing his or her students' letter–sound knowledge on an ongoing basis and re-teaching letters to selected children when necessary.

An excellent small-group activity that can be used to review (and assess children's retention of) previously taught letter-sounds is to have children sort picture cards into categories by beginning consonant sound. First, the children take turns sorting a dozen or so words (pictures) into three columns by beginning sound alone.

Next, letter cards are brought out, and the children sort the words according to the beginning consonant sound–letter match (*mop* is placed under *m* because its first sound is /m/.)

Finally, the teacher dictates six sounds (e.g., /b/, /s/, /m/) or six words (*bear, sock, moon*) and has the children write the corresponding letter for each.

If the task sequence above (sorting by beginning consonant sound, sorting by letter–sound match, and writing letters to dictation) is used to review three letter-sounds, it might be completed in one lesson. On the other hand, if the sequence is used to introduce three new letter-sounds, it may take a full week of lessons to move the children successfully through the three tasks (For fuller descriptions of beginning consonant sorts, see Bear, Invernizzi, Templeton, & Johnston, 2000; Morris, 1999.)

Awareness of the beginning consonant in isolated words is an important starting point; however, it is the application of this knowledge in contextual reading that is the ultimate goal.

During a reading lesson, if a child hesitates or misreads a word in sentence context, the teacher has available a simple, effective option. *Without saying a word, he or she can point to the beginning consonant letter in the misread word, signaling the child to use this cue as he or she attempts to read the word.* On occasion, the teacher may have the child return to the beginning of the sentence and use the sentence context plus the beginning consonant cue to help identify the target word. Although easy to use, this teaching strategy is extremely important. It demonstrates to kindergarten readers that, within a contextual reading situation, beginning consonant knowledge can be a helpful word recognition aid.

Another simple but quite effective technique involves the teacher covering (with an index card) a single word in an oft-repeated dictation or big book and having the children guess what letter the "mystery" word begins with, for example,

> We made popcorn.
> We made it in a popper.
> We put butter and ___?___ on the popcorn

To do so, first the children must use the story and sentence context to identify the target word (in this case, *salt*). Then they must think about the beginning sound in the "mystery" word (/s/) and identify the letter that represents that sound (s). At this point, the children will eagerly await the teacher uncovering the first letter in the mystery word and, on seeing it, will be justifiably proud of their problem-solving ability. This little game, played two or three times per week, can have a dramatic effect on children's tendency to use beginning cues in their contextual reading. (Note that, later in the school year, the same game can be used to focus children's attention on ending consonant sounds.)

The above discussion of beginning consonant letter–sound instruction has ushered in the important topic of *phoneme awareness*. It is certainly true that beginning readers must be able to attend to individual sounds (phonemes) in words before they can match letters to these sounds. Nonetheless, many reading educators wrongly equate phoneme awareness with full segmentation ability, that is, the child's ability to attend to each sound in a spoken word (e.g., /bĭt/ = /b/ + /ĭ/ + /t/). Instead, phoneme awareness is a complex, multilayered understanding that develops slowly over time. First, children become aware of the initial consonant sound in words (the /b/ in /bĭt/), later, the initial and ending sounds (/b/ – /t/), and, finally, the consonants and the medial vowel (/b/ /ĭ/ /t/) (Ehri, 1998; Lewkowicz, 1980; Morris & Perney, 1984). At the outset, then, it makes good sense to prioritize beginning consonant discrimination and teach it right along with the alphabet (see instructional examples above).

Rhyme is another aspect of language awareness that should be addressed in kindergarten. Informal word play and games, poetry, even Dr. Seuss books can be effective in drawing young children's attention to rhyming elements in spoken words (e.g., /r-ăt/, /b-ăt/, /c-ăt/; /b-āk/, /m-āk/, /c-āk/; or /b-ē/, /m-ē/, /w-ē/). Note, however, that attention to rhyme does not necessarily lead the child to segment each phoneme in the syllable or word. The /-ăt/ in /răt/ and the /-āk/ in /bāk/ are unsegmented chunks in which the vowel is not separated from the ending consonant. Therefore, with regard to phoneme segmentation, attention to rhyme is more an entry point than a final destination.

Beyond beginning consonant discrimination and rhyme, phoneme awareness or segmentation can be taught in different ways. Some psychologists and educators advocate a direct, oral approach in which children are provided with explicit training in segmenting spoken words into phonemes. Over several months' time, the teacher guides students in segmenting first, two-phoneme words (e.g., /ăt/ = /ă/ /t/) and later, three- and four-phoneme words (e.g., /săt/ = /s/ /ă/ /t/; /flăt/ = /f/ /l/ /ă/ /t/). Several studies (e.g., Ball & Blachman, 1991; Blachman, Ball, Black, & Tangel, 1994; Bradley & Bryant, 1983) have reported gains in young children's reading and spelling ability when explicit phoneme segmentation training is paired with letter–sound instruction.

A less direct approach to developing phoneme segmentation ability is to engage young children in supported reading and writing activities and allow the writing system itself to teach them about the phonemic properties of words. For example, as kindergarteners finger-point read and reread simple texts (e.g., dictations and big books), they come to learn, with the teacher's guidance, how spoken words match to printed words (Clay, 1991; Morris, 1993) and how printed words are composed of letters that match to sounds (Holdaway, 1979; Morris, 1993). If these same children are simultaneously taught the alphabet letters (and corresponding sounds), then they can begin to write their own texts. And early writing, as we will see in the next section, is not only a purposeful language arts activity, but also an ongoing exercise in attending to phonemes within spoken words.

Early Writing

The linguist Carol Chomsky (1971) once stated that children should "write first, read later." In analyzing preschoolers' written messages, Chomsky had observed that young children often construct or spell words by attending to the sequential sounds in the words. Thus, a precocious five-year-old might write:

I	YET	FOR	A	RID	EN	DA	KR
(I	went	for	a	ride	in	the	car.)

Chomsky reasoned that early writing can be an important precursor to reading acquisition because it provides prereaders with purposeful experience in analyzing the sequence of sounds in spoken words and in matching appropriate letters to these sounds (see Adams, 1990; Clay, 1991; Ehri, 1989; Richgels, 2001).

Following Chomsky's logic, kindergarten teachers should emphasize writing in the curriculum. At the beginning of the year, group-dictated experience stories can be used to model the writing process. As the teacher records the dictated story, word by word, on chart paper, the children learn that we write from left to right, that printed words are separated by spaces, and that a period is placed at the end of the sentence. The teacher can also focus the children's attention on letter sounds by having them predict what letter comes first in the next word to be written in the story (e.g., "Our next word is *principal*. What letter should I write first?" [A child responds] "Good, Mary, the first letter in "principal" is *p*.")

> *School Trip*
> We visited the cafeteria.
> We visited the first graders.
> We visited the p _____ .

After a month or so of school, kindergarteners should be encouraged to write their own texts. At first, their task might be to draw a picture and write a caption underneath. As the children begin to work, the teacher (and possibly an aide or parent) circulates through the room, helping individuals write their caption sentence. For those children who lack alphabet knowledge, the teacher acts as a scribe, writing down the child's dictated caption and helping him or her read it back. For other children who can write some alphabet letters, the teacher helps them attend to individual letter-sounds in words. In the writing sample below, Curtis hesitated when he reached the third word in his sentence, *takes*. In supporting Curtis, the teacher says, "Curtis, what's the first sound you hear in *takes*? [Child says /t/.] "Good! What letter makes that sound?" [Child says *tee*.] "Good, write it down."

M	D	T	M	T	S
(My	dad	takes	me	to	school.)

In another writing sample (see below), Mary had no difficulty writing beginning consonants; however, initially that is all she wrote. In supporting and extending Mary's writing effort, the teacher says, "Mary, you heard the first sound in *dog* and wrote a *d*. Say *dog* slowly. What comes after the *d*?" [Child says /daw—g/ – /g/.] "Good! What letter should we put down?" [Mary writes a *g*.] The same probe is repeated successfully with *can* and *flies* and the teacher provides the tricky *-ch* in *catch*.

M	DG	CN	CCH	FS
(My	dog	can	catch	flies.)

Notice in these examples that the act of writing led the children naturally to attend to individual sounds within words. Notice also that when the teacher provided assistance—probing for additional sounds—she was actively teaching phoneme awareness.

With guided practice over a few months' time, kindergarteners' writing ability will improve. They will enjoy writing about family, friends, pets, cartoon favorites, holidays, after-school experiences, and so on. By midyear, discussion of a shared class experience (e.g., playing in the snow at recess) can serve as a stimulus, not just for dictation, but for independent writing. For example,

Sarah

W	P	N	D	S
(We	played	in	the	snow.)
I	H	F		
(I	had	fun.)		

Jack

I	PD	IN	THE	SNO	WF	JAMES
(I	played	in	the	snow	with	James.)
I	MD	A	SNOBL			
(I	made	a	snowball.)			

Kim

ME	AND	CAROL	MAD	A	SNOWMAN
(Me	and	Carol	made	a	snowman.)
WE	MAD	HIS	BODE	AN	HAD
(We	made	his	body	and	head.)
HE	IS	VARE	LEDL		
(He	is	very	little.)		

In February, the kindergarten teacher is proud that Sarah, Jack, and Kim can write independently, and can produce written coherent messages using their knowledge of letter–sound correspondences. The teacher is also aware of the diagnostic information embedded in the children's spellings. He or she realizes that Sarah is writing with beginning consonants only (P for *played*; S for *snow*; H for *had*); that Jack is representing both beginning and ending consonants (PD for *played*; WF for *with*; BL for *ball*); and that Kim is representing consonant boundaries and the medial vowel in her spellings (MAD for *made*; BODE for *body*; LEDL for *little*). Thus, we see that kindergarten writing samples, aside from their message quality, can yield useful information about individual children's developing phoneme awareness.

Summation

In the preceding discussion, the elements of a kindergarten reading program (reading stories aloud, guided contextual reading, letter–sound work, and early writing) were discussed separately. And, in fact, some kindergarten teachers may choose to designate a separate part of the school day for each activity; for example, contextual reading first thing in the morning, writing and letter–sound work at midmorning, and reading to the children in the early afternoon. Still, it should be apparent by now that these literacy activities are integrally related to each other. By listening to stories read aloud, children develop vocabulary and a concept of story, as well as an overarching purpose for learning to read and write. The knowledge children gain through finger-point reading dictations and big books (e.g., attention to the spoken word–written word match, beginning consonant cues, sight vocabulary, etc.) is applied in their own sentence and story writing. Conversely, the letter–sound knowledge that they exercise in writing is applied in their reading. Even the seemingly isolated work on the alphabet and letter–sound correspondences is immediately put into practice each time the children read a story or invent spellings in a writing activity. The result is an integrated literacy program that melds whole-to-part and part-to-whole learning in a meaningful way.

One should also keep in mind that the daily reading/writing activities are easily integrated into the broader kindergarten curriculum. Specific stories read aloud by the teacher can be chosen to match content themes (e.g., mammals, weather, Thanksgiving) being studied by the class. And shared classroom experiences (e.g., discussions, experiments, field trips) can regularly be preserved in written language via dictated stories and writing activities. In truth, this was one of the original goals of the language-experience approach (Stauffer, 1970): to enable children to use language to capture and interpret ongoing, meaningful experience.

Assessment and Its Instructional Implications

Beginning-of-Year Assessment

- Child writes his/her name.
- Child names the upper- and lower-case alphabet letters.

Kindergarten teachers have a lot on their minds the first few weeks of school, and a formal assessment of student reading ability is not usually high on the priority list. Nonetheless, as the children begin to settle into classroom routines, a few informal assessments can provide the teacher with valuable information. For example, observation of each kindergartener attempting to write his or her name yields information about alphabet letter knowledge, letter orientation, and fine-motor coordination (Bloodgood, 1999). The teacher will also want to assess how many upper- and lower-case alphabet letters the child can identify when the teacher points to them in random order (see Appendix, Part 1). This assessment provides an important baseline measure of alphabet knowledge for each child.

Other aspects of beginning kindergarteners' literacy-related knowledge can be assessed quite reliably through informal observation. For example, does the child speak in clearly articulated sentences or in indistinct short phrases? Does his or her early writing include scribbles, numbers, pictures, alphabet letters or a combination of these? If alphabet letters, do they indicate a logical letter–sound match (e.g., I LMTR for *I like my teacher*)? Does the child settle in and show interest when the teacher reads a storybook aloud to the class? Can he or she answer questions about the story? Does the child pay attention when the teacher records a dictated experience story on the chalkboard? Following the teacher's model, can the child finger-point read the first sentence in the dictated story? Such off-the-cuff observations early in the school year are invaluable to the teacher in setting realistic expectations and planning meaningful instruction for individual children.

Mid-Year Assessment

- Child names and writes the lower-case alphabet letters.
- Child finger-point reads a four-sentence story.
- Child spells six words.

Effective teaching of beginning reading and writing requires ongoing, informal assessment by the teacher. On a daily basis, the teacher instructs (or models), observes and evaluates children's reading behavior, and then adjusts future instruction accordingly. Based on overall student performance, the teacher may decide to move forward (e.g., introduce a new and more difficult big book), remain at the same instructional level (reread the current big book or introduce a new one of similar difficulty), or drop back and review at an easier level (revisit big books that were introduced and completed several weeks earlier).

Over a few months of observing children in group and individual contexts, a knowledgeable kindergarten teacher (Ms. Green, for example) will have an idea about each child's literacy development. Those children most prominent in Ms. Green's mind will be the few, perhaps a half-dozen in a class of twenty-two, who seem to be falling behind the group in reading and writing achievement. To Ms. Green, it seems that her whole-class literacy instruction (and follow-up individual assistance) has not been sufficiently intense to drive the reading/writing development of these low achievers.

Therefore, sometime between mid-November and early January, Ms. Green decides to provide pull-out or small-group instruction to her lowest readers, children whom she considers to be at-risk. To ensure that she is selecting the children who are most in need of the small-group help, Ms. Green informally assesses the ten lowest readers in her class. Her assessment, which takes about ten minutes per child, includes three tasks:

- *Alphabet knowledge.* The child names the lower-case alphabet letters as the teacher points to each in random order (see Appendix, Part 1). Then the child writes the letters as the teacher dictates them one by one. Ms. Green is especially interested in the child's knowledge of those alphabet letters that have been introduced in her class over the first three months of the school year.

- *Concept of word in text.* In an echo-reading format (teacher reads first, then child reads), the child finger-point reads a four-sentence story (see Appendix, Part 2). After reading each sentence, the child attempts to identify individual words within the sentence when the teacher points to the words.

- *Spelling.* The child attempts a "sound-it-out" or phonemic spelling of six words (*back, feet, step, junk, road,* and *dig*). The teacher pays close attention to the number of phonemes the child can represent in his or her spelling attempts (see Appendix, Part 3).

The results of Ms. Green's mid-year assessment support her informal observations and document that six children in her class are in need of extra help. On average, these six children know only one third of the fifteen alphabet letters that have been introduced, are inconsistent in finger-point reading, and cannot represent even beginning consonants in their spelling attempts.

Small-Group Instruction.   Ms. Green begins meeting with her small group of low readers for twenty-five minutes on Monday, Wednesday, and Friday. In these sessions, she uses a set lesson plan:

- *Contextual reading.* The teacher leads the six children in choral reading a big book or favorite dictated story that was introduced to the whole class earlier in the school year. Then, individual children attempt to read portions of the text and to identify specific words and letter sounds in the text. The teacher provides help as needed.

- *Letter–sound work.* The children take turns sorting words (pictures) by beginning consonant sound and matching consonant sounds to the appropriate letter. They also practice writing alphabet letters to dictation. Game formats (e.g., Memory, Bingo) are used to maximize attention and learning.

- *Writing.* The children write short sentences dictated by the teacher (e.g., "I like to color."). At first they concentrate on representing beginning sounds in words (I L T C); later, they are able to represent both beginning and ending sounds (I LK TO CLR).

The small-group lessons, for the most part, review content (stories, letter sounds) and procedures (rereading, sorting, writing) that were previously introduced in the whole-class setting. This reduces teacher planning time and lends a comforting air of familiarity to the lessons ("We've seen this before."). Nonetheless, it is the small-group setting itself that allows the children to succeed. Here they can receive, three times per week, carefully structured, teacher-guided opportunities to read and write. And, with time and opportunity, they progress. After two months of small-group lessons, Ms. Green finds that two of her six charges have begun to "catch on;" that is, they finger-point read with ease, spell with both beginning and ending consonants, and even know a few sight words. She decides to graduate these two youngsters and to move another child into the small group. Ms. Green continues small-group lessons with her five neediest students over the final three months of the school year. The children's progress is slow, but the teacher recognizes and values each small step forward.

End-of-Year Assessment

- Child names upper- and lower-case alphabet letters, and writes lower-case letters to dictation.
- Child finger-point reads a four-sentence story.
- Child spells six words.
- Child reads a list of ten isolated words.

The kindergarten reading instruction described in this chapter has focused on contextual reading, letter–sound correspondences, and the use of writing to develop phoneme awareness. By the end of the school year, kindergarten children ideally should be able to name and write the alphabet letters, finger-point read simple texts, represent at least beginning and ending consonant sounds in their spelling attempts, and recognize a few frequently occurring sight words. An individual child's ability to do this can be assessed using four simple tasks: *alphabet knowledge, concept of word in text, spelling,* and *word recognition.* Recall that the first three tasks were administered to a subset of children at midyear to help identify those in need of small-group assistance. Now, at the end of the year, the teacher will want to administer the four-task battery to all students in order to document their achievement. (*Note:* Specific directions for administering the tasks are found in the Appendix, Parts 1–4.)

Analyzing End-of-Year Performance. On the *alphabet* task, the child names the upper-case letters and then the lower-case letters as the teacher points to them in random order. The child also writes the lower-case letters as the teacher dictates them in random order. By the end of kindergarten, the child should be able to name twenty-two or more of the lower-case letters. A score of 18 to 21 is marginal, and the child who can name seventeen or fewer lower-case letters may be at risk as he or she enters first grade (Morris & Perney, 1997).

On the *concept-of-word-in-text* task, the child finger-point reads four sentences (4 points) and attempts to identify two target words within each sentence when the examiner points to the words (8 points). A child with a firm grasp of the spoken word–written word match in reading should score 10 or higher on this twelve-point task. A score of 7 to 9 indicates a marginal grasp of the concept, and a score of 6 or lower may indicate guessing behavior.

On the *spelling* task, the child attempts a sound-it-out spelling of six words dictated by the teacher. The six words (*back, feet, step, jump, road,* and *dig*) include twenty possible sounds or phonemes. Administered at the end of kindergarten, the spelling task is an excellent predictor of reading success in first grade (Mann, Tobin, & Wilson, 1987; Morris & Perney, 1984; Stahl & Murray, 1994). This is because sound-it-out spellings allow children to demonstrate their phonemic awareness—their ability to attend to the sequence of sounds within spoken words. Table 2.1 shows how four kindergarteners might score on the spelling task.

Referring to the table, John has difficulty representing even beginning consonants in his spellings;. Mary represents beginning consonants only; Robert represents both beginning and ending conosonants; and Brenda, the most advanced speller, represents consonant boundaries and the vowel element. On this spelling (or phoneme awareness) task, a score of 12 and above is good; 8 to 11 is adequate; 4 to 7 is marginal; 3 or below is at risk.

On the *word recognition* task, the child attempts to read five frequently occurring sight words (*is, me, cat, and,* and *the*) and five decodable words (*pin, lap, met, job, nut*). A score of 5 or higher on this ten-word test indicates that the child can probably read simple stories. However, even if the child fails to read any of the words correctly, important information can be gleaned from his or her word-reading attempts. For example, does the child even attempt to read the word? Does he or she decode or "sound" the first letter (/p/ for *pin*)? Does a misreading preserve the beginning and ending consonants in the word ("pan" for *pin*; "meet" for *met*)?

Table 2.2 shows the performance of four representative kindergarteners on the end-of-year assessment. Note that Brenda and Robert achieved passing scores on the alphabet, concept of word and spelling tasks, and could read a few words on the word-recognition task. Mary achieved a passing alphabet score, but only marginal scores on concept of word and spelling. She was unable to read any words on the word recognition task. Finally, John, whom the kindergarten teacher is considering for retention, scored well below criterion on each task. He is clearly at risk for

TABLE 2.1 *Four kindergarteners' performance on the spelling task*

	John	*Mary*	*Robert*	*Brenda*
back	B	B	BK	BAC
feet	—	F	FT	FET
step	S	S	SP	SAP
jump	—	J	GP	JOP
road	—	R	RD	ROD
dig	—	D	DG	DEG
Total	2	6	12	18

TABLE 2.2 *Four kindergarteners' performance on the end-of-year assessment*

Child	Alphabet (26)	Concept of word (12)	Spelling (20)	Word Recognition (10)
Brenda	25	12	18	3
Robert	24	10	12	1
Mary	22	8	6	0
John	15	4	2	0

Note: Passing criteria are as follows: *alphabet* = 22 of 26; *concept of word* = 10 of 12; and *spelling* = 8 of 20. There is no criterion for *word recognition.*

reading difficulties if promoted to the first grade in the fall. This record of children's print-related knowledge serves two important purposes: (1) It provides feedback to the kindergarten teacher regarding the effectiveness of her instructional program; and (2) It provides the first-grade teacher (next year's teacher) with valuable information regarding individual children's print-related knowledge.

Children will, of course, mature and change in small ways over the summer between kindergarten and first grade. Some will forget, some will get "rusty," and some (particularly those from literacy-rich homes) may even advance their reading skill. Still, the difference between a May kindergartener and an August first grader is only three months. For this reason, we will see, as we move to the next chapter, that there is continuity between the reading instruction and assessment offered to children at the end of kindergarten and that offered to them at the beginning of first grade.

References

Adams, M. (1990). *Beginning to read: Thinking and learning about print.* Cambridge, MA: MIT Press.

Ball, E., & Blachman, B. (1991). Does phoneme awareness in kindergarten make a difference in early word recognition and developmental spelling? *Reading Research Quarterly, 26,* 49–66.

Bear, D., Invernizzi, M., Templeton, S., & Johnston, F. (2000). *Words their way: Word study for phonics, vocabulary, and spelling instruction.* Columbus, OH: Merrill.

Blachman, B., Ball, E., Black, R., & Tangel, D. (1994). Kindergarten teachers develop phoneme awareness in low-income, inner-city classrooms. Does it make a difference? *Reading and Writing: An Interdisciplinary Journal, 6,* 1–17.

Bloodgood, J. (1999). What's in a name? Children's name writing and name acquisition. *Reading Research Quarterly, 34,* 342–367.

Bradley, L., & Bryant, P. (1983). Categorizing sounds and learning to read: A causal connection. *Nature, 30,* 419–421.

Bus, A., van Ijzendoorn, M., & Pellegrini, A. (1995). Joint book reading makes for success in learning to read: A meta-analysis on intergenerational transmission of literacy. *Review of Educational Research, 65,* 1–21.

Chomsky, C. (1971). Write first, read later. *Childhood Education, 47,* 296–299.

Clay, M. (1991). *Becoming literate: The construction of inner control.* Portsmouth, NH: Heinemann.

Cowley, J. (1980). *Mrs. Wishy-washy.* Auckland, NZ: Shortland.

Donaldson, M. (1978). *Children's minds.* New York: Norton.

Ehri, L. (1989). Development of spelling knowledge and its role in reading acquisition and reading disabilities. *Journal of Learning Disabilities, 22,* 356–365.

Ehri, L. (1998). Grapheme-phoneme knowledge is essential for learning to read words in English. In J. Metsala & L. Ehri (Eds.), *Word recognition in beginning literacy* (pp. 3–40). Mahwah, NJ: Erlbaum.

Ehri, L., & Wilce, L. (1985). Movement into reading: Is the first stage of printed word learning visual or phonetic? *Reading Reseach Quarterly, 20,* 163–179.

Holdaway, D. (1979). *Foundations of literacy.* Auckland, NZ: Heinemann.

Huey, E. B. (1908). *The psychology and pedagogy of reading.* New York: Macmillan. (Republished in Cambridge, MA: MIT Press, 1968.)

Lewkowicz, N. (1980). Phoneme awareness training: What to teach and how to teach it. *Journal of Educational Psychology, 72,* 686–700.

Mann, V., Tobin, P., & Wilson, R. (1987). Measuring phonological awareness through the invented spellings of kindergarten children. *Merrill-Palmer Quarterly, 33,* 365–391.

McGill-Franzen, A. (1992). Early literacy: What does "developmentally appropriate" mean? *Reading Teacher, 46,* 56–58.

Morris, D. (1993). The relationship between children's concept of word in text and phoneme awareness in learning to read: A longitudinal study. *Research in the Teaching of English, 27,* 133–154.

Morris, D. (1999). *The Howard Street tutoring manual: Teaching at-risk readers in the primary grades.* New York: Guilford.

Morris, D., & Perney, J. (1984). Developmental spelling as a predictor of first-grade reading achievement. *Elementary School Journal, 84,* 441–457.

Morris, D., & Perney, J. (1997). *Predicting which children will succeed in an early reading intervention program.* Paper presented at the annual meeting of the National Reading Conference. Scottsdale, AZ.

Richgels, D. (2001). Invented spelling, phonemic awareness, and reading and writing instruction. In S. Neuman & D. Dickinson (Eds.), *Handbook of early literacy research* (pp. 142–155). New York: Guilford.

Routman, R. (1988). *Transitions from literature to literacy.* Portsmouth, NH: Heinemann.

Snow, C., Burns, S., & Griffin, M. (1998). *Preventing reading difficulties in young children.* Washington, DC: National Academy Press.

Stahl, S., & Murray, B. (1994). Defining phonological awareness and its relationship to early reading. *Journal of Educational Psychology, 86,* 221–234.

Stauffer, R. (1970). *The language-experience approach to the teaching of reading.* New York: Harper & Row.

Templeton, S. (1997). *Teaching the integrated language arts.* Boston: Houghton Mifflin.

Wells, G. (1986). *The Meaning Makers.* Portsmouth, NH: Heinemann.

Appendix

1. *Alphabet task*

Recognition: The child names the alphabet letters, upper- and lower-case, as the teacher points to them in random order (Score = 0 to 26 for upper-case recognition and 0 to 26 for lower-case recognition). *Production:* The child writes the alphabet letters as the teacher dictates the letter names in random order. The child can write either the upper- or lower-case form of the alphabet letter (Score = 0 to 26). The randomized alphabet chart below can be used for both the recognition and production task.

A	F	P	W	K	Z	B
C	H	O	J	U	Y	M
D	L	Q	N	S	X	I
G	R	E	V	T		

a	f	p	w	k	z	b
c	h	o	j	u	y	m
d	l	q	n	s	x	i
g	r	e	v	t		

2. *Concept of word task*

The child and teacher read together the four-page "Katie" book (see following page). Turning to page 1, the teacher says:

> The sentence down here [pointing to the first printed sentence, "Katie is . . ."] tells what is happening in the picture. I am going to point to each word as I read; then I want you to point to each word as you read. [The teacher finger-point reads the sentence.] Now it's your turn. [Child attempts to finger-point read.]

On completion of the child's finger-point reading attempt, the teacher immediately points to the first target word (*rain*) [see chart below] and asks, "Can you read this word? and then points to the second target word (*walking*) and asks, "What about this one?"

	Point	Words
2 1* 1. Katie is *walking* in the *rain*.	_____	1 _____ 2 _____
1 2 2. *She* sees a *big* dog.	_____	1 _____ 2 _____
2 1 3. The *dog* shakes *water* on Katie.	_____	1 _____ 2 _____
2 1 4. "You *are* a very *bad* dog!"	_____	1 _____ 2 _____

*In each sentence, note carefully the order in which the teacher points to the target words.

After recording the child's responses on the first sentence, the teacher moves to the second, third, and fourth sentences, repeating the same procedure on each.

The score sheet is filled in as each sentence is completed. Finger-point reading attempts are scored in an all-or-nothing (+ or −) manner. That is, *the child receives credit only if he/she points to and reads correctly each word in the sentence* (self-corrections are acceptable). The child can receive a score from 0 to 12 on the concept-of-word task: 4 finger-point reading attempts and 8 word identification attempts.

Katie is walking in the rain.

She sees a big dog.

The dog shakes water on Katie.

"You are a very bad dog."

3. *Spelling task*

The teacher begins by modeling a sound-it-out spelling of the sample word, *mat:*

> We are going to write the word *mat.* What letter should I write down first? [The teacher offers praise for the correct response, *m,* and writes the letter down. If the student gives the wrong letter or fails to respond, the teacher still writes the letter *m* on the paper.] *M* is the first letter in *mat.* What letter should we write down next? (and so on.)

With the sample spelling completed, the teacher hands the pencil to the child, and says:

> Now, I'm going to call out some more words, and I want you to try and write them. Remember, for each word, think about what letter comes first, what comes next, and so on. Okay, the first word is *back."*

During the six-word spelling test, the teacher pronounces the words clearly; he or she does not exaggerate or elongate the sounds in the words.

The list of six spelling words, along with scoring examples, is shown in the chart below. Four of the spelling words contain three sounds or phonemes (*back*, *feet*, *road*, and *dig*) and two of the words contain four sounds (*step* and *jump*). Total score on the test is the number of sounds (0 to 20) that the child represents in his or her spellings. For detailed explanations of the phonetic appropriateness of a given letter (e.g., C for S in the CP spelling of *step*; E for I in the DEG spelling of *dig*), see Morris (1999) or Morris and Perney (1984).

Spelling Word	1 point	2 points	3 points	4 points
1. back	B, BN	BC, BK, BA, BIK	BAC, BAK, BACK	
2. feet	F, FA	FT, FE, FOT	FET, FETE, FEET	
3. step	S, C, SO	ST, CP,* SE, SA	STP, SDP, SAP, CEP	STAP, SDAP, STEP
4. jump	J, G	JP, GP, JO, GU	JOP, GOP, JUP, JMP	JOMP, GUMP, JUMP
5. road	R, RW	RD, RO	ROD, ROAD	
6. dig	D	DG, DE	DEG,* DIG	

4. *Word-recognition task*

The child attempts to read ten words as the teacher points to them one at a time. The first five words are frequently occurring sight words, and the last five are short-vowel, decodable words (Score = 0 to 10).

1. is	6. pin
2. me	7. lap
3. cat	8. met
4. and	9. job
5. the	10. nut

3

Reading Instruction in First Grade

Darrell Morris

How reading should be taught in first grade has been and continues to be one of the most controversial topics in elementary education. The topic is controversial for good reasons. First of all, there is a great deal at stake. Children who fall behind in reading in first grade have difficulty catching up with their peers (Clay, 1991a; Juel, 1988; Stanovich, 1986), and those who are still behind in third grade are seriously at risk in an educational system that, from fourth grade on, demands grade-level reading ability. Second, there is the problem of teaching a vital "tool" skill to individuals in a large-group context (first-grade classrooms contain eighteen to twenty-four students). Fraatz (1987) called this the "paradox of collective instruction," the fact that first-grade teachers must provide reading instruction for everyone, while simultaneously addressing individual differences among their students. Third, learning to read and teaching beginning reading are complex skills, leading to professional uncertainty and considerable debate about both learning process and teaching method. The psychologist, Charles Perfetti (1985), summed it up this way:

> Reading is both simple and complex. It is at the same time both cognitively trivial and so difficult that failure at learning to read is common . . . Countless parents with no expertise in reading can boast of their preschool children's prodigious accomplishments in literacy . . . However, not all children are so lucky. Many children do so poorly at reading that they are given a special category, 'developmental dyslexia.' Moreover, quite aside from specialized reading disabilities, there is continuing widespread concern about the ordinary failures of reading experienced by countless numbers of children who never earn the "dyslexic" label . . . (p. 3)

Interestingly, at the turn of the twenty-first century there is some consensus in the reading field regarding the critical components of the learning-to-read process.

Researchers (e.g., Adams, 1990; Snow, Burns, & Griffin, 1998; Stanovich, 1998) agree that beginning readers must learn to (1) attend to individual sounds within words, (2) decode printed words by matching letters to sounds, and (3) automatize decoding or word-level processing so that the mind can concentrate on the meaning of what is being read. But identification of the component parts of a complex process does not necessarily dictate the order in which these parts should be taught to children. Based on the evidence, a researcher (e.g., Lyon, 1998) might advocate what appears to be a logical instructional sequence: phoneme awareness → decoding → fluency → comprehension. However, an experienced first-grade teacher might believe that comprehension (or a focus on meaning) should be emphasized from the very start. The same teacher might argue, from experience, that early reading and writing activities need not await, but can actually facilitate young children's phoneme awareness (see Chomsky, 1979; Morris, 1993). Thus, while the components of the reading acquisition process are important and not to be ignored, how they are ordered and orchestrated in the act of teaching children to read has been, is, and always will be the subject of debate.

In this chapter on first-grade reading instruction, I attempt to avoid a debate on reading methods—what some have called the "reading wars" (e.g., phonics emphasis vs. literature-based vs. "balanced" instruction). Historically, there have been no real winners in this arena, only shifts in the line of battle (some large, some small) every decade or so. Instead, I focus on broader issues that confront all first-grade teachers of reading, for example:

- assessing early reading ability
- providing for individual differences
- acquiring a set of carefully graded reading materials (early first to mid-second grade)
- developing an effective small-group instructional routine
- guiding children's contextual reading
- teaching word recognition
- pacing reading instruction efficiently
- documenting end-of-year reading achievement

Although I focus on the broad issues above, the specifics of my discussion will undoubtedly offend purists on both sides of the beginning reading debate. So be it. My intended audience is the vast middle—those teachers (and administrators) who are entrusted with the important, day-to-day responsibility of teaching six-year-olds to read.

Issues in First-Grade Reading Instruction

Assessing Early Reading Ability

To assess children's reading ability during the first week of school, the first-grade teacher can use the same assessment battery that was used at the end of kindergarten (see Appendix in Chapter 2, p. 29). This individual assessment contains four tasks (alphabet, concept of word in text, spelling, and word recognition) and takes only ten minutes to administer. Table 3.1 shows variation in student performance on the assessment battery in a typical first-grade class.

The scores in Table 3.1 suggest three groupings of beginning readers:

• The top eight scorers (Karen through Billy) have strong alphabet knowledge, finger-point read with accuracy, represent beginning and ending consonants as well as a few vowels in their spellings, and recognize a small number of first-grade words.

• The middle seven scorers (J.J. through John) have fairly complete alphabet knowledge, show an emerging ability to finger-point read, represent beginning and ending consonants but not vowels in their spellings, and show little word recognition ability.

TABLE 3.1 *Student performance on a beginning-of-first-grade reading assessment.*

	Alphabet (Lower-case)	Concept of Word in Text	Spelling (Phon. Aware.)	Word Recognition
Student	26	12	20	10
Karen	25	12	19	5
Mandy	24	12	18	3
Lindsay	25	11	18	3
Eli	25	9	17	2
Steven	23	7	16	3
Michael	25	12	16	2
Allison	24	11	16	1
Billy	24	10	15	2
J.J.	24	9	13	1
Brenda	24	9	12	0
Leslie	24	6	11	1
Zeb	21	9	8	0
Derrick	21	7	8	0
Connie	22	7	9	0
John	23	6	9	0
Carolyn	21	6	6	0
Mary	20	3	4	0
Cecil	19	4	3	0
Bobby	19	5	3	1
Rita	18	4	2	0
Lucas	16	2	2	0
David	14	2	1	0

- The lowest seven scorers (Carolyn through David) have gaps in their lower-case alphabet knowledge, are inconsistent in matching spoken words to printed words when reading, represent, at best, beginning consonants in their spellings, and cannot read words in isolation.

On first look, these scores might suggest three distinct reading groups in this first-grade class. But the teacher must exercise judgment. For example, do J.J. and Brenda belong in the top group or the middle group? Does Carolyn belong in the middle or the low group? Fortunately, teachers can gather other data to help them make such decisions. Daily, informal observations of the children in various literacy activities will tell teachers which children can finger-point read, which can spell with both beginning and ending consonants, and which can recognize a few sight words. Such observations will also reveal important information about individual children's motivation, attention, and oral language development. It is the combination of informal assessment and ongoing observation of children's literacy behavior that can provide teachers with a reliable picture of their students' reading ability at the beginning of first grade.

Providing for Individual Differences

Attending to individual differences while providing instruction to everyone is the considerable challenge facing first-grade teachers of reading. Historically, teachers have used reading ability groups or small-group instruction to address this challenge (Barr, 1995; Slavin, 1987). The major advantage of grouping is that it allows children possessing similar reading skill (e.g., high, middle, or low readers, see Table 3.1) to read stories and study word patterns at the appropriate difficulty level. Another advantage is that, in the act of reading a story or doing a skill activity, a small group (as opposed to the whole class) affords children more opportunities to interact with the teacher and the teacher more chances to observe the performance and assess the understanding of individual children (Stauffer, 1970; Tharp & Gallimore, 1988).

Unfortunately, there are problems associated with reading ability groups. First, some educators believe that children's self-esteem can be harmed by placement in a low-reading group (Barr, 1995). Second, children who are "locked into" a low-reading group placement across several grades can fall significantly behind their peers in reading (Hiebert, 1983; Juel, 1988). Third, the very practice of ability grouping presents classroom teachers with significant organizational and management problems, such as, "What do I do with the children who are not with me in the reading circle?"

One can acknowledge the potential problems associated with ability grouping, yet still favor the practice in the primary grades. In teaching children to read (particularly those who struggle with the process), there is no substitute for having them, on a daily basis, read stories and study word patterns at the appropriate difficulty level. For most first-grade teachers, only a well-planned grouping scheme can make this possible. Below I describe two approaches to grouping first graders for reading instruction: grouping same-level readers within a heterogeneous class-room and grouping same-level readers across several first-grade classrooms.

Grouping within a Classroom. Once early reading ability has been carefully assessed and children assigned to reading groups, a teacher might adopt the following daily schedule (see Figure 3.1). Reading instruction begins each day with a whole-class literature circle. During this thirty-minute period (8:30 to 9:00 A.M.), all children in the class join the teacher in choral-reading big books and poems, composing and reading dictated stories, and listening to stories read aloud. This opening period is a prioritized time for building community through the sharing of classroom experiences and good literature.

The next 30 minutes (9:00 to 9:30 A.M.) is devoted to writing workshop, a time when the teacher circulates among the children as they start, continue, or bring to completion self-chosen pieces of writing.

Reading groups come next (9:30 to 10:45 A.M.). One group of children goes to the reading circle for teacher-guided instruction (both story reading and word study); a second group returns to their desks to complete a seatwork activity; and a third group divides up and goes to one of three *centers* (e.g., listening, word study, drawing/writing) where the children complete a pre-assigned task. After twenty-five minutes, the teacher rings a bell, and the groups rotate: children in the reading circle go to seatwork, those at seatwork go to centers, and those at centers go to reading circle (see Figure 3.2). There is a third and final rotation of the groups.

8:30–9:00 A.M.	**Whole class literature circle.** Teacher leads children in choral reading big books and poems, and in writing and reading dictated stories; the teacher also reads aloud good books to the class.
9:00–9:30 A.M.	**Writing workshop.** The children write on self-selected topics while the teacher circulates, providing support and encouragement as needed.
9:30–10:45 A.M.	**Reading groups.** Teacher meets with students in small ability-leveled groups in which stories are read and discussed, and letter-sounds and word patterns studied. While the teacher is engaged with a reading group, the other children complete seatwork assignments or work at designated learning centers. (9.30 to 9:55 A.M.—Group 1; 9:55 to 10:20 A.M.—Group 2; 10:20 to 10:45 A.M.—Group 3)
10:45–11:05 A.M.	**Self-selected reading.** The children, back at their seats, read self-selected books, either independently or with a partner. The teacher conferences with individual children regarding their reading choices.

FIGURE 3.1 *A daily schedule for first-grade reading and writing instruction.*

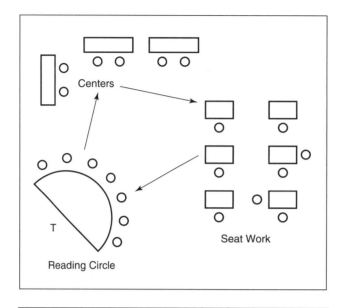

FIGURE 3.2 *Rotation of reading groups in a first-grade classroom*

When reading groups end, the children return to their seats to read self-selected books, either independently or with a partner. The teacher uses this final twenty minutes of "free-reading" (10:45 to 11:05 A.M.) to conference with individual children and listen to them read aloud.

One purpose of this schedule is to give the teacher approximately twenty-five minutes of instructional time with each ability group. (*Note:* As the year progresses, the teacher may find that the low group requires a little more guided reading time whereas the top group requires a little less.) To gain this valuable small-group time, however, the teacher must plan carefully and train the children to work independently when they are away from the reading circle at their seats or at the centers (see Fountas & Pinnell, 1996, for specific ideas about managing such a classroom). Because teaching reading with rotating groups is a formidable task, teacher aides or parent volunteers can be of enormous assistance with management. Also, some schools have experimented with split-class scheduling of special activities (e.g., music, gym, foreign language, etc.) to facilitate reading instruction. With this plan, one half of the children in each of two first-grade classrooms go to gym at the same time each day; the other half remain in the classroom. This gives each teacher thirty minutes to instruct only ten or so students in reading. When the first gym period is over, the children switch places (gym students return to their classrooms, the other children go to gym), and each teacher has another thirty-minute period to teach reading to ten students.

Grouping across Classrooms. Another way to group first graders by reading ability level is to group across classrooms. Let us say there are sixty-six children in three heterogeneously grouped first-grade classrooms. An initial reading assessment reveals that twenty-five of the children can be classified as high readers, twenty-three as average, and eighteen as low. Therefore, during the morning reading period (ninety minutes), the twenty-five high readers go to Teacher A's room, the twenty-three average readers to Teacher B's room, and the eighteen low readers to Teacher C's room. At the conclusion of the reading period, all the children return to their home classrooms.

The major advantage of this across-class grouping scheme is that it greatly reduces the variability in student reading skill facing each teacher. With twenty-five relatively strong readers, Teacher A can do some whole-group lessons and possibly divide his or her children into two reading groups instead of three. Teacher B may be able to do the same. Teacher C does face a difficult task in teaching the eighteen lowest first-grade readers. However, if the school reading teacher co-teaches this low group with Teacher C (and what could be a better use of the reading teacher's time?), then two teachers would be responsible for only eighteen students across a ninety-minute period. They could group and regroup these low readers as they saw fit and, given this context, the possibilities for quality small-group instruction and individualized help would be high.

When considering across-class grouping, we should keep several things in mind. First, the assignment of a presumably "same-level" group of readers to a given teacher does not necessarily eliminate the need for further grouping of these students. For example, there could easily be stronger and weaker readers within the so-called middle reading group assigned to Teacher B. Moreover, Teacher B may at times want to regroup her "middle-group" students in order to have small discussion groups within her class; discussing a story with seven children is quite different from discussing it with a class of twenty-three. A second consideration is that the teacher of the low group (see Teacher C, above) should always receive the smallest number of students. Low readers require much reading practice and individual feedback from the teacher if they are to progress. And third, in an across-class grouping scheme, every effort should be made to make reading-group membership as flexible as possible. Thus, if a few children in the low group start to "catch on" to reading after a few months of instruction, they should immediately be given a chance to move up to the middle group.

Acquiring a Set of Carefully Graded Reading Materials

Historically, the classroom materials used to teach beginning reading have been provided by the large basal reader publishers (e.g., Ginn, Harcourt Brace, Houghton Mifflin, Scott Foresman, etc.). Over the years, these publishers, bowing to trends in scholarship and politics, have changed not just the content but the form of first-grade reading materials. For example, basal readers of the 1950s and 1960s (e.g., Scott Foresman's "Dick and Jane") featured strict word control or the systematic repetition of a core vocabulary across stories and book levels. The word-control basals were modified in the 1970s and 1980s to include much more phonics instruction. In the 1990s, both word control and phonics were greatly deemphasized as the whole-language movement ushered in the new literature-based basal readers (Hoffman et al., 1994). As we enter the new millennium, a strenuous reaction in opposition to whole-language instruction is producing yet another type of first-grade basal, one that attempts to straddle the chasm between phonics-controlled or decodable text and the more natural language text characteristic of children's literature.

Despite significant changes in basal readers over the past fifty years, a majority of first graders have learned to read while a sizeable minority (perhaps 30 percent) have struggled with the process. From this, one could question whether reading materials themselves really make that much difference. I strongly believe that they do, particularly for those children who require careful teaching if they are to learn to read. For these children, however, it may not be the type of reading material that is crucial (i.e., word-control, phonics-emphasis, natural-language, or a combination), but rather the degree to which the material is carefully graded in difficulty and matched to their level of reading skill.

Over the past ten years, two first-grade reading intervention programs—Reading Recovery (Pinnell, Lyons, Deford, Bryk, & Seltzer, 1994; see Chapter 4) and Success for All (Slavin, Madden, Karweit, Dolan, & Wasik, 1994; see Chapter 5)—have proven successful in helping at-risk children learn to read. Importantly, both programs employ a large set of carefully graded reading materials. Reading Recovery uses natural-language text while Success for All uses decodable text, but both programs include ten or more text difficulty levels within the first grade (many more levels than are found in classroom basal readers). This careful leveling of stories in both programs allows the tutor to place the student at the appropriate "instructional level" and to pace him or her gradually but efficiently through the graded reading curriculum.

If a carefully leveled set of books is critical in teaching at-risk beginning readers in a tutorial context, it is equally critical in teaching these children in the classroom. But the discomforting and truly difficult-to-understand fact is that many first-grade teachers do not have access to such a graded set of reading materials. The first-grade stories in the 1990s basals were not carefully graded in difficulty because, in the whole-language era, literary quality took precedence over repetition of a core vocabulary. It remains to be seen if the first-grade basals of the current decade (2000–2010) will achieve a consistent gradient of story difficulty as they navigate between decodable text in the preprimers and more conventional text in the later first-grade levels (primer and late first grade).

This is not a new problem. Arthur Gates (1969) argued thirty years ago that a single basal reader program would not meet the needs of every child in a classroom. He argued for multiple sets of graded materials, with the teacher deciding which materials to use with different groups of children. Dr. Gates's recommendation still makes good sense. However, to follow his advice, today's first-grade teachers (with the support of their principals and school districts) will have to exercise careful judgment in purchasing reading materials. I suggest the following guidelines:

- Early in the year, use big books and language-experience stories to teach children basic print concepts, such as left-to-right directionality, the spoken word–written word match, use of beginning consonant cues, and an initial sight vocabulary.
- When basic understandings have been established, place children in carefully controlled text to help them build sight vocabulary and develop decoding skill. These preprimer texts might be sight-word based, phonics-based, or predictable in nature. The important points are (1) that the texts be carefully graded in difficulty, with a sufficient number of selections at each difficulty level, and (2) that they engage children's interest.
- On reaching the primer or mid-first-grade reading level, the more able readers in a first-grade class will be able to read basal stories and tradebooks that are somewhat variable in readability or word control. These children are decoding new words, retaining sight words with minimal repetition, and developing what Clay (1991a) called a "self-improving system." On the other hand, average and struggling first-grade readers, on reaching the primer level, still require some structure and control in their reading materials. The repetition of sight words and spelling patterns across stories, as well as some consistency in sentence length, can be instrumental in helping this group progress. Carefully leveled tradebooks (e.g., Random House's *Step into Reading* series or Harper and Row's *I Can Read* series) can be effective at this mid-to-late first-grade reading level, but keep in mind that a series of tradebooks—each written by a different author in a different style—do not always provide sufficient word repetition and syntactic consistency across stories. Ironically, the best place to find such built-in language support for average to low readers is in the primer and 1–2 levels of the traditional basal readers of the 1970s and 1980s, materials that are no longer in print.

Developing an Effective Small-Group Instructional Routine

In a whole-class setting, the first-grade teacher can read aloud to children, model the reading and writing processes on the chalkboard, and facilitate meaningful discussion on a variety of topics. Nonetheless, a *small-group* setting affords the teacher a better opportunity to guide the reading development of individual children. In a small group, six to eight children can read and discuss an appropriately leveled text in the presence of a supportive teacher each day. The teacher, in turn, can closely monitor the children's word-reading accuracy and comprehension, providing encouragement and corrective feedback as needed. Just getting a class of twenty-four six-year-olds to the point where small-group instruction is possible—where the teacher can work for twenty-five minutes with a subgroup of eight children—is a significant managerial task (see discussion on grouping, p. 37). But management is just the first step. The teacher must then follow through with effective instruction within the small groups. Such instruction will include routines for guiding contextual reading and teaching letter–sound relationships and spelling patterns.

Guiding Children's Contextual Reading. At the beginning of first grade, the teacher can use big books and dictated experience stories to review basic print concepts (e.g., the spoken word–written match, beginning consonant cue use) and help children acquire an initial sight vocabulary (see Johnston, 2000). Such instruction can be done in the whole-class setting and/or in small reading groups. Soon enough, however, the teacher will want to place the students in a set of graded reading materials and advance them through these materials with all deliberate speed.

Jump forward to the sixth week of school. Envision a small circle of seven or so children around the teacher, with each child holding a copy of a simple printed story (the story could be from a basal or a popular tradebook series). The teacher's challenge—or paradox, if you will—is how to support children in reading a text when they lack the sight vocabulary needed to do so. For many years, first-grade teachers have addressed this problem by using a small-group procedure called "round-robin" reading. Starting on page one, one child in the group takes a turn reading aloud two or three sentences, his or her peers following along as best they can. Then another child takes a turn, and another and another, until the story is completed. The teacher provides word-recognition support as needed and checks the children's comprehension of the story at regular intervals. Unfortunately, with struggling readers, teacher assistance with word recognition is needed on nearly every line. This often leads to a tedious reading lesson, characterized by a stumbling, self-conscious performance by the child who is reading aloud, and inattention by those who are supposedly following along. Its weaknesses notwithstanding, round-robin reading has survived over the years for commonsense reasons: (1) It provides a routine for managing the group (i.e., one child takes a turn reading while the others follow along, then another child takes a turn); (2) It provides children with supervised oral reading practice; and (3) It provides daily opportunities for the teacher to assess the reading progress of individual children.

Critics of the round-robin reading procedure abound, but surprisingly few have put forth concrete, carefully worked-out alternatives. In this section, I offer one alternative, *supported oral reading* or SOR (see Chapter 5 for another alternative). SOR is a small-group teaching routine (Morris & Nelson, 1992) that can be adapted for use in first or second grade. An amalgam of two ideas, Hoffman's (1987) "oral recitation lesson" and Clay's (1991b) "story introduction," SOR cycles over a three-day period.

Day 1. Previewing and echo reading. The teacher and children preview the first eight to ten pages of the selection, discussing the pictures on each page and making predictions about the story line (e.g., "What is happening in this picture? What's going to happen next? [turning to the next page] Now what is happening?"). The teacher may redirect the children if their predictions are off the mark. During the preview or "picture walk," the teacher also points to and identifies a few words in the text that the children may find difficult to decode. Done appropriately, the preview provides children with a set of expectations, a mental outline to be filled in as they begin to read the story.

Next, the teacher and children return to the beginning of the story and proceed to *echo read* one page at a time. In the echo procedure, the teacher orally reads a page (two or three sentences) slowly, but with correct phrasing and intonation. Then the children mumble-read the same page, finger-pointing to each word. The teacher provides word-recognition assistance when needed. At various points in the story, the teacher stops and checks on comprehension (e.g., "Why did the giant grab the little elf?" or "What do you think will happen next in the story? Why?"). These comprehension stops help to structure the lesson and provide purpose to the echo reading. (*Note:* To add challenge to the Day 1 reading, the teacher can increase the amount of text he/she reads [e.g., two pages instead of one] before having the children echo read.)

Day 2. Partner reading.   The six or eight children in the small group are paired up at their seats, a "strong" reader with a "weak" reader. The children reread the entire Day 1 story, alternating pages with their partners; that is, one child reads pages 1, 3, 5, and so on and the other child reads pages 2, 4, and 6. The teacher moves from pair to pair during this partner-reading, monitoring the children's on-task behavior and providing encouragement and support as needed.

Next, each child is assigned a part of the story for concentrated practice (perhaps the first or second half of the story, approximately one hundred words). One child reads his assigned part to his partner, and then she reads her part to him. The children are encouraged to help each other when help is needed.

Day 3. Expert reading.   During their small-group time, the children come back to the teacher, one by one, and read their assigned part (one hundred words). The teacher acts as a diagnostician during this reading, *providing no help unless the child is stuck or refuses to go on.* The teacher makes a mark (/) in her notebook for each word recognition error: substitution, omission, insertion, or help. Children who can read their passage with 97 percent accuracy or better can put a star on their individual story chart; those who read with at least 93 percent accuracy can put a circle on their chart.

An alternative form of Day 3 expert reading involves reassembling the small group and having the children round-robin read the story, which is well practiced by now. The emphasis is on accurate, expressive oral reading, and again the teacher takes informal measures on each child's reading performance.

Over time, as first graders develop sight vocabulary and become more independent in reading, the teacher can modify the SOR procedure for Day 1. For example, in working with the low-reading group in December, the teacher might guide the children's reading of a twelve-page, late-preprimer story in the following manner:

- briefly preview the first few pages of the story
- return to the beginning and lead the children in echo reading only the first two pages

- have individual children read aloud the next four pages (have the group make predictions about what will happen next)
- have the group read silently (or mumble-read) the next three pages (make predictions about how the story will end)
- have the group read the last three pages silently, and then discuss the story's outcome

Note in this example that the teacher has cut back on echo reading (or memory support) in order to provide the children with word-recognition challenge. Also note that Day 1 of SOR has evolved into a comprehension lesson or directed reading–thinking activity (see Templeton, 1997), with the emphasis on active reading guided by the students' predictions. On Day 2, partner-reading of the same story could be used to enhance the children's reading fluency and build their confidence.

In summary, supported oral reading is an adaptable, small-group reading routine. It offers needed support to beginning readers who are struggling with word recognition, and it can help more able first-grade readers improve their comprehension and reading fluency. Although SOR is offered as only one of many possible alternatives to small-group round-robin reading, I believe that any critic would do well to consider the teacher's roles in SOR; for example, guiding story comprehension, modeling fluent contextual reading, monitoring children's rereadings of a given story, and providing each child with a final opportunity to show his/her mastery of the story.

Teaching Word Recognition. Most first-grade readers need help in the area of word recognition. Providing such help, however, is not a simple, straightforward task. First, the teacher must understand the content or developmental continuum of word-study instruction (e.g., beginning consonants, word families, short-vowel patterns, long-vowel patterns, etc.). Second, he or she must be able to determine where individual students need to be instructed along this continuum. And third, the teacher must develop a method or procedure for teaching the various letter–sound relationships and spelling patterns.

Content. There is agreement on what constitutes the basic content of a first-grade word-study program (see Calfee, 1982; Gray, 1960; Henderson, 1990). Textbooks often recommend a sequence like the one shown in Figure 3.3. In the figure, think of each element in a given column as representing a particular word pattern. For example, -at in the word-family column might stand for *hat, mat, cat,* and *flat; big* (short *i*) in the short-vowel column might stand for *big, hit, fin,* and *clip;* and *lake* in the vowel-pattern column might stand for *lake, made, race,* and *plane.*

The sequence of instruction depicted in Figure 3.3 moves from left to right. In fact, a child's learning of concepts further along the continuum (e.g., long-vowel patterns) will depend, in large part, on his or her mastery of concepts introduced earlier (e.g., word families, short vowels). To this end, there is overlap built into the instructional sequence that facilitates the learner's movement from one conceptual level to the next. For example, mastery of *beginning consonants* prepares the child for

Beginning consonants	Word families*	Short vowels*	One-syllable vowel patterns	
b	-at	a hat	(a)	mat
c	-an			lake
d	-ap			park
f	-ack			tail
g				
h	-it	i big	(i)	kid
j	-in			ride
k	-ig			bird
(etc.)	-ick			light
ch	-ot	o top	(o)	job
sh	-op			rope
th	-ock			coat
wh				born
	-ed	e pet	(e)	leg
	-et			seed
	-ell			meat
				he
	-ut	u rub	(u)	bug
	-ug			mule
	-ub			burn
	uc/c			suit

FIGURE 3.3 *Sequence of word study instruction*

*Consonant blends (bl, dr, st, etc.) are introduced at the word-family and short vowel levels.

word-family sorts. Proficiency in reading and spelling the short-vowel rhyming words (*word families*) leads naturally into work on the five short-vowel patterns. And mastery of the *short-vowel words* ensures that the child will bring important knowledge to the one-syllable vowel-pattern stage. Thus, there is a developmental logic to a good word-recognition curriculum, a logic that is sometimes not fully understood in theory nor fully implemented in practice.

Placement on the Continuum. Just as a child has an "instructional level" in contextual reading, he or she also has one in word recognition. Effective word study must take into account what the student knows about words. Aiming instruction too low (e.g., teaching beginning consonants when the child already knows these letter–sound features) wastes time and effort. Aiming too high (e.g., teaching long-vowel patterns to a child who does not understand the basic short-vowel CVC patterns) can

Spelling word	Bobby	Brenda	Eli
back	B	BK	BAK
feet	—	FT	FET
step	S	SP	SAP
jump	—	GP	JP
road	R	RD	ROD
dig	B	DG	DEG

FIGURE 3.4   *Spelling performance of three first graders on beginning-of-year assessment*

produce frustration and, worse, confusion. Fortunately, it is not difficult to assess a beginning reader's level of word knowledge, particularly if we think in terms of broad conceptual levels (see Figure 3.3) instead of discrete skills.

A good way to begin is to analyze children's invented spellings. Figure 3.4 shows the spelling performance of three first graders on the beginning-of-year assessment (see *Assessing early reading ability,* p. 34). Note, in the figure, that Eli represents beginning and ending consonants and the medial vowel in his spellings (e.g., SAP for *step*); Brenda represents beginning and ending consonants only (SP); and Bobby represents, on occasion, the beginning consonant (S). These children are obviously functioning at different conceptual levels and their word-study instruction should be adjusted accordingly. Bobby needs beginning consonant instruction. Brenda and Eli could benefit from short-vowel word family instruction, though Eli, given his superior vowel awareness, will probably progress more quickly through the word families.

These are preliminary judgments of course. As the teacher begins to work with the children in small groups, he or she will gain a better understanding of Bobby, Brenda, and Eli's respective strengths and weaknesses in the area of word recognition.

An Instructional Method.   Given individual differences in children's word knowledge, we believe that word recognition (or phonics) should be taught in the small reading group, along with guided reading. In this way, low, average, and high readers can learn letter–sound relationships and spelling patterns at the appropriate developmental level. There are, of course, many ways to teach word recognition. In this section, I describe a word categorization or "word sorting" method that was developed at the University of Virginia in the 1980s and popularized in the recent textbook, *Words Their Way* (Bear, Invernizzi, Templeton, & Johnston, 2000; also see Henderson, 1990; Morris, 1999). My intent, however, is not to advocate a particular method but to illustrate the developmental course of word study across a school year.

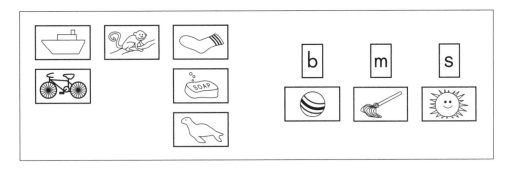

FIGURE 3.5 *Examples of beginning consonant sorts: (left panel) sorting by beginning sound and (right panel) sorting beginning sound to letter*

At the beginning of the school year, the seven children in Bobby's low-reading group learn to discriminate *beginning consonant sounds* in words, an important, rudimentary form of phoneme awareness. First, they practice sorting picture cards into columns by beginning consonant sound (see Figure 3.5). Then they attend to the sound–letter pairings (/b/ = *b*; /m/ = *m*; /s/ = *s*). As the children master the beginning consonant letter–sound relationships, the teacher encourages them to use this knowledge (to attend to the beginning consonant) in contextual reading and writing.

With the beginning consonants mastered, the reading group proceeds to *short-vowel word families*. This is a long and productive stage (two to three months) in which the children study the five short vowels, one at a time, in a rhyming-word format. A typical activity might involve the group sorting twelve short *a* words into three rhyming patterns. The teacher begins by arraying three header words on the table. The children *must* be able to read these headers.

hat   *man*   *cap*

Next, the teacher models how to sort one or two short *a* words under the appropriate header. He or she demonstrates that a new word (e.g., *sat*) can be read by referring to the header (*hat–sat*).

hat	*man*	*cap*
sat	ran	

Finally, the children take turns sorting the remaining word cards, reading down the column each time they sort a word.

hat	*man*	*cap*
sat	ran	map
rat	pan	tap
flat	can	trap

Once the group gains facility in sorting and reading the words in column format, the teacher introduces activities (Memory, Bingo, Go Fish, Spell Checks) that provide the children with practice in reading and writing the short *a* words in isolation. On completion of the short *a* word families (this may take several weeks), the teacher introduces short *i* families (*hit, win,* and *pig*), followed by short *o*, short *e*, and short *u* families, in that order. Consonant blends (e.g., *bl-, dr-,* and *st-*) and digraphs (e.g., *ch-, sh-,* and *th-*) are introduced early (with short *a* and *i*) and practiced throughout the word-family phase of instruction.

Word-family sorts are used as the vehicle for early word study because, after beginning consonants, we consider them to be the easiest entry into word analysis. Given a known word (e.g., *can*), the child can read a new, unknown word (*pan*) by simply changing the initial consonant (/c/ to /p/) and then blending the consonant (/p/) with the rhyming vowel-consonant ending (/an/). Most beginning readers find this to be a doable task and, in the context of daily column sorts, word games, and spell checks, they steadily develop sight vocabulary and decoding facility. That is, they learn to read many short-vowel words at sight (e.g., *cat, fan, sit, top,* etc.) and to decode or "sound out" others (*clap, tip, fed, shop,* etc.) that are not sight words.

For those few children who struggle with decoding, even given the word-family support, a fall-back instructional position is to have them "make" or construct words by moving letter-chips on the table (see Figure 3.6). For example, the teacher might say to a child, "Make the word *mat;* now make *mad;* now *bad;* now *bag;* now *big.* Or, better still, the teacher might move the letters around and have the children take turns reading a sequence of teacher-constructed words (see Morris, 1999). "Make-a-word," it should be noted, always takes place in the context of the specific short vowels being studied, for example, *a* and *i*. In this way, the teacher can provide the children with both an analytic (word-family sorts) and a synthetic (making words) route to improving their recognition of short-vowel words.

Following extensive work on the short-vowel families, *vowel patterns* are introduced in the small group. The first vowel-pattern sort provides a review as the

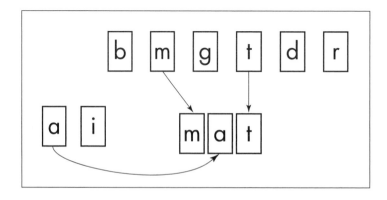

FIGURE 3.6 *"Making words" with individual letters: A short vowel lesson*

children sort short-vowel words into non-rhyming, consonant-vowel-consonant (CVC) patterns.

hat	*big*	*top*
mad	win	pot
bag	sit	job
clap	trip	rock

Later vowel-pattern sorts, usually introduced in the second half of the year, present more complex contrasts; for example, *short vowel* (CVC) versus *long vowel* (CVCe) versus *r-controlled* (CV-r) patterns:

bat	*make*	*hard*
ran	name	car
pad	late	park
flag	trade	start

On completing the *a* patterns (again, this may take one or two weeks), the group works on *i* patterns (e.g., *hit, ride,* and *girl*), and then on *o, e,* and *u* patterns in that order. There is no rush, and the emphasis is on mastery of each set of vowel patterns.

Different reading groups (low, middle, and high) will progress at different speeds through the first-grade word-study sequence outlined above. This is as it should be. As the year goes along, some children, who start out in a lower reading group, may advance to a higher group and thus to a higher word-study level. The consistency of the word-sorting procedure across reading groups should facilitate such changes in group membership.

In summary, word study or phonics instruction, when paced appropriately by the teacher, helps first-grade readers master the high-frequency short- and long-vowel patterns. Given this foundation, the children can begin to make sense of other spelling patterns they come upon in contextual reading. In a sense, good phonics instruction should highlight or "bring into focus" critical spelling patterns that are within the learner's developmental grasp (Henderson, 1990; Invernizzi, Abouzeid, & Gill, 1994). Then, purposeful reading and writing can drive the patterns into memory, leading to the important goal of fluent reading.

Pacing Reading Instruction Efficiently

Pacing refers to the first-grade teacher's skill in guiding (or moving) his or her students through a set of graded reading materials. The concept is extremely important because the farther children progress in the first-grade reading curriculum, the higher their reading achievement at the end of the year. All things being equal, the student who is reading in the late first-grade book (1–2) in May will be a stronger reader than the student who is still reading in the primer (1–1). In a carefully conducted field study, Barr (1974, 1982) found that four factors tended to influence first-grade teachers' pacing of reading instruction: (1) difficulty of the classroom reading materials; (2) time allocated to reading instruction; (3) number of low readers in the classroom; and (4) the teacher's years of experience teaching first grade. Although Barr's study was conducted some years ago in classrooms where traditional, word-control basal readers were being used, I believe her findings to be as relevant today as they were then.

In Barr's study (1974), different first-grade basal reader programs were used in different schools. The more difficult programs, according to Barr, introduced reading vocabulary and phonics concepts at a faster rate than did the less difficult programs. Thus, the difficult programs featured less repetition of a core vocabulary across first-grade reading levels and less practice or review of basic phonics concepts. While a challenging, concept-loaded basal program may enhance the achievement of high-ability readers, it can overwhelm low-ability readers who need a slow, measured introduction of new concepts and much review if they are to progress. This is, in fact, what Barr found. First-grade teachers who used a "difficult" basal were less successful in pacing their low readers through the first-grade reading curriculum.

Instructional time was a second factor that influenced pacing in Barr's study. Put simply, the more time the teachers spent directly instructing the children in reading, the farther the children advanced in the basal reader program. Because instructional time is a variable that teachers can manipulate, Barr suggested that teachers consider meeting with the low-reading group a second time each day (e.g., in the afternoon) to help accelerate this group's reading progress. (*Note:* One-to-one tutoring outside the classroom also increases instructional time for low readers: see Chapter 4.)

A third factor that influenced instructional pacing was the number of low-readiness or low-ability readers in a first-grade classroom. The larger the number of struggling readers in the classroom, the more difficulty the teacher had in pacing them through the reading program. This makes sense. Low readers in a group of eight, as opposed to a group of four, can take only half as many turns reading aloud and half as many turns sorting word cards in the presence of the teacher. Half as much reading practice and half as much teacher instruction each day will, over the year, make a huge difference in achievement. Barr also pointed out that behavior problems tend to be found among low-readiness children, and the teacher who has more than one or two "acting-out" children in a first-grade classroom is often forced to spend an inordinate amount of time managing behavior.

The final influence on pacing that Barr identified was the number of years the teacher had spent teaching first grade. Teachers possessing more first-grade experience tended to be more successful in advancing their students through the first-grade reading program. Effective, experienced first-grade teachers know where their children need to be reading by the end of the school year. These teachers assess their students' reading on an ongoing basis and move individuals forward (e.g., to a higher reading group) when they are ready for additional challenge. Finally, these first-grade teachers have a thorough understanding of their reading materials, knowing which stories and skills to emphasize, which to move through quickly, and which to skip. Thus, effective pacing—advancing beginning readers as fast as they can go—boils down to goal orientation, ongoing assessment, flexible grouping, and the efficient use of classroom reading materials.

Before leaving the issue of instructional pacing, let us consider, for illustrative purposes, a worst-case and a best-case example. In the worst-case example, Ms. Ward, a first-year teacher, is assigned a first-grade class in which nine of her twenty-two students are low-readiness or at risk. The only reading materials in the young teacher's room are a difficult 1990s basal reader that features little word control in the early levels and a supplemental phonics program that is characterized by step-by-step tedium. Finally, Ms. Ward has only ninety minutes each day to teach reading and language arts, and this time period is interrupted by a morning gym class three days per week.

In our best-case example, Ms. Ball, a first-grade teacher with eight years of experience, is assigned a class of twenty-two students, only five of whom could be classified as low-readiness. This teacher has accumulated three sets of reading materials over the years and plans to use them, as needed, with her low-, middle-, and high-reading groups: (1) a brand new 2001 basal reader that features controlled, decodable text in the early levels; (2) an older 1990s literature-based basal; and (3) multiple copies of a set of carefully graded early first-grade tradebooks from the Wright Group and Rigby series. Ms. Ball has an uninterrupted 120 minutes each morning to teach reading and language arts.

In these two examples I have "stacked the deck" to show that low readers have a much better chance of learning to read in Ms. Ball's class than in Ms. Ward's class. Ms. Ball is an experienced first-grade teacher who has adequate materials and time to meet the individual needs of a small number of low readers in her class. In contrast, Ms. Ward's context—her own inexperience, a large number of low readers, inappropriate materials, and inadequate time—makes teaching reading very difficult. The hypothetical nature of these examples notwithstanding, I believe that there are far too many first-grade classrooms in the real world that approximate Ms. Ward's. School boards, principals, and teachers need to work together to make sure that the pacing factors identified by Rebecca Barr work in favor of, not to the detriment of, first-grade children. In short, this means striving to make first-grade classrooms look more like Ms. Ball's and less like Ms. Ward's.

Additional Pieces of the Puzzle

Although I have concentrated on small-group reading instruction in this chapter, there are other areas of instruction that are crucial in getting first graders off to a good start in reading. Among these are writing, independent or free reading, and reading aloud to children.

Writing is an important language art that deserves a chapter or book of its own (see Cramer, 2001, or Temple, Nathan, Temple, & Burris, 1993). But writing also plays a role in children's learning to read. Therefore, I advocate daily writing (twenty to thirty minutes) based on the process model originally described by Graves (1983). First graders should write, for the most part, on self-chosen topics; use invented spellings to help express their ideas; share their in-progress drafts with their classmates and teacher; and, with the teacher's help, publish their best work (see Chapter 5: *Writing from the Heart*).

From a reading perspective, writing in the early months of first grade can help children develop phoneme awareness: the understanding that words are composed of a sequence of individual sounds that match to letters (see Chapter 2, p. 19; also Chomsky, 1979; Clay, 1991a). As the year progresses, writing allows first-grade readers to assume the stance of an author; it affords them continual opportunities to read and reread text (both their own and that produced by classmates); and it provides children a purposeful arena for experimenting with, practicing, and eventually internalizing letter-sounds, spelling patterns, and sight words.

For the teacher, children's writing leaves a permanent trace that can not only be appreciated and responded to, but also analyzed. Figure 3.7 shows a writing sample produced by a first-grade boy in January. He was attempting to retell the fable, "The Lion and the Mouse," which had been read aloud to his class on the previous day. Notice that the child's writing sample reveals a good sense of story, an ability to sequence ideas, and an expressive style (spar me, I'm too litl for you to eit). He spells correctly the words that he knows (e.g., *time, was, mouse, big, out*, etc.) and invents other spellings in a developmentally appropriate manner (e.g., SLEPIN for *sleeping*; WAN for *when*; KAM for *came*; KLMD for *climbed*; RAR for *roar*, etc.). Finally, he seems to be blissfully unaware (at least on first drafts) of the need for punctuation and capitalization. From this single example, we can readily see that there is a wealth of diagnostic information to be gleaned from children's writing.

Independent or free reading is another activity that should be emphasized in a first-grade literacy program. Because reading improves the more one reads, first graders' reading experience should not be limited to the small-group reading circle. Instead, they should engage in self-selected reading during a designated inde-

---

The Lion and the Mouse

Oans a pan a time thar was a lion that was
slepin on the groun wan (when) a mouse kam
out of hes hol and klmd (climbed) over the lion.
the lion lat [out] a big rar (roar) the mouse sad (said)
spar me I'm to lilt for you to eit I'll halp you if
you dont [eat me] 7 mons want [by] the lion got
kot (caught) in a trap the lion let a big rar the mouse
rak in nis (recognized) the vos he wat (went) to the
spot He chod (chewed) a hol in the net and the lion said,
I'm not going to col (call) enebode (anybody) to litl to halp.

FIGURE 3.7 *Writing sample produced by a first grader in January*

pendent reading period (twenty minutes in the morning or afternoon), at their seats when they have completed assignments, and at home. At the beginning of first grade, self-selected reading is a bit problematic because not all the children can read independently, and some, who can read, lack the ability to choose books of appropriate difficulty. To address this problem, the teacher can level (or color-code) all reading materials in the classroom according to difficulty level. Then, during independent reading, the teacher can guide individual children to a shelf of books (e.g., red = beginner; blue = preprimer; green = primer; and yellow = late first grade) that will provide appropriate challenge. For first graders with very limited reading ability, the independent reading period offers a chance to *reread* (with another student or the teacher) big books, dictated stories, or tradebooks that were introduced to the class earlier in the day or week. This same pattern applies to take-home reading. More able first-grade readers, using the color-coding system, can self-select books to take home and read with their parents; less able readers will benefit from taking home previously introduced books and rereading these texts with their parents.

Along with writing and independent reading, the teacher reading aloud to the class should be a staple of the first-grade literacy curriculum. Only by listening to books read aloud can young children begin to sense the special cadence of written language and learn to construct and sustain meaning across pages of text (see Chapter 2, p. 9; also Wells, 1986). By reading to the class on a daily basis, the teacher is preparing children for the increasingly complex texts they themselves will be reading as they advance through the elementary grades. First- and second-grade teachers usually choose narratives, both classic and contemporary, as read-aloud material. However, they should also begin to read information books to their students. Pappas (1991), among others, has made a strong case that kindergarteners and first graders need consistent exposure to non-narrative or expository genres if they are to be successful with the content or subject-matter reading that awaits them in the mid-elementary grades.

Documenting End-of-Year Reading Achievement

After a first-grade teacher has assessed and grouped his or her students, acquired a set of reading materials, developed a balanced instructional routine, and paced the students efficiently through a graded reading curriculum, the teacher will, at year's end, want to document how much the children have learned. Such assessment information can be shared with parents, the school principal, and, importantly, next year's teachers. In this section I describe an end-of-year reading assessment that has been used successfully in Early Steps, an intervention program for at-risk first-grade readers (see Morris, Tyner, & Perney, 2000; Santa & Hoien, 1999). The individual assessment, which takes fifteen to twenty minutes to administer, includes three tasks: word recognition, passage reading, and spelling (see Appendix).

In the *word recognition* task, the child attempts to read a list of forty words, graded in difficulty from early first grade to mid-second grade (see Appendix, Part 1). If the child is unable to read a word within three seconds, the examiner moves on to the next word. Testing continues until the child misses seven words in a row. One point is awarded for each word read correctly. A score of *30* and above indicates a late first-grade reading level; *22* to *29* indicates a primer reading level; *14* to *21* indicates a late-preprimer reading level; and *13* and below indicates an early-pre-primer reading level.

In the *spelling* task, the child attempts to spell a list of fifteen words. Each of the fifteen words is scored according to a developmental rubric devised by Morris and Perney (1984). This scoring system (see Appendix, Part 2), which assigns 0 to 5 points per word, takes into account both phonemic and orthographic properties of children's spellings. For example, the following spellings of *feet* receive 1 to 5 points, respectively: F (1 point), FT (2 points), FET (3 points), FETE (4 points), and FEET (5 points). Total score on the fifteen-word test can range from 0 to 75. A score of *55* and above indicates strong, late first-grade word knowledge (correct short vowels and marked long vowels); a score of *40* to *54* indicates mid to late first-grade knowledge (at minimum, the ability to represent the sequential sounds in a word); and a score of *39* and below indicates early to mid first-grade word knowledge (most likely some difficulty in representing medial vowels).

In the *passage reading* task, the child reads aloud up to six passages that progress in difficulty from early first grade to late second grade (see Appendix, Part 3). The final four passages (primer, late first grade, early second grade, and late second grade) contain one hundred words each. The child begins reading at Level 1 and progresses through as many passages as he or she can. As the child reads aloud, the examiner keeps a running record of errors made (substitutions, omissions, insertions, examiner helps) and time needed to complete the passage. The examiner discontinues the passage reading if the child's oral reading falls below 85 percent accuracy on the second passage (preprimer 2) or below 90 percent accuracy on one of the later passages (primer and above). The child's score, ranging from 0 to 6, equals the highest passage reading level attained.

The end-of-year assessment described above affords three different looks at first graders' reading ability. Although the passage reading score is the most important, the other two scores (word recognition and developmental spelling) correlate highly with passage reading and provide a reliable measure of beginning readers' word knowledge. Administered with care, this three-task assessment will provide valid documentation of children's reading ability at the end of first grade.

First-grade teachers do not, of course, wait till the end of the school year to assess reading ability. They informally assess their students' reading and writing on an ongoing basis throughout the year. For example, to help with pacing decisions (i.e., whether to move a child to a lower or higher reading level), the first-grade teacher, on occasion, takes one-hundred-word samples of individual students' oral reading behavior. If the child reads the passage with 95 percent accuracy or better, the teacher may decide to move him or her to a higher reading level. A score of 90 to 94 percent accuracy indicates that the child's current reading level is appropriate, and a score below 90 percent accuracy may indicate that he or she is overplaced in reading. The teacher also regularly monitors students' writing to determine when they make conceptual advances in word knowledge; for example, to see when a first-grade writer begins to represent short vowels conventionally (DRES instead of DRAS for *dress*) or begins to mark long vowels with an extra vowel letter (FETE instead of FET for *feet*). For a more uniform assessment of reading ability (perhaps at midyear), a first-grade teacher could administer to each student in the class one or more of the tasks (word recognition, spelling, passage reading) described in this section. Such an assessment would provide valuable information regarding students' midyear reading ability and a valid prediction or estimate of their end-of-year reading ability (see Morris & Perney, 1984).

Conclusion

In this chapter I have addressed basic issues that confront all first-grade teachers of reading (e.g., assessment, grouping, materials, teaching methods, and pacing). Although these are "backbone" issues that must be attended to, there is much more involved in teaching a class of twenty-two first graders to read. William James (1899) said it well one hundred years ago:

> I say moreover that you make a great, a very great mistake, if you think that psychology, being the science of the mind's laws, is something from which you can deduce definite programs and schemes and methods of instruction for immediate school room use. Psychology is a science, and teaching is an art; and sciences never generate arts directly out of themselves. An intermediate, inventive mind must make the application by using its originality (p. 3).

At best, the content of this chapter provides a starting point: a reasonable framework for beginning to think about effective first-grade reading instruction. To carry out such instruction, to teach a classroom of children to read, requires "an intermediate, inventive mind"; it requires a knowledgeable, empathic, hardworking teacher.

References

Adams, M. (1990). *Beginning to read: Thinking and learning about print.* Cambridge, MA: MIT Press.

Barr, R. (1974). Instructional pace differences and their effect on reading acquisition. *Reading Research Quarterly, 9,* 526–554.

Barr, R. (1982). Classroom reading from a sociological perspective. *Journal of Reading Behavior, 14,* 375–389.

Barr, R. (1995). What research says about grouping in the past and present and what it suggests about the future. In M. Radencich & L. McKay, (Eds.), *Flexible grouping for literacy in the elementary school* (pp. 1–24). Boston: Allyn & Bacon.

Bear, D., Invernizzi, M., Templeton, S., & Johnston, F. (2000). *Words their way: Word study for phonics, spelling, and vocabulary* (2nd ed.). Columbus OH: Merrill.

Calfee, R. (1982). Literacy and illiteracy: Teaching the nonreader to survive in the modern world. *Annals of Dyslexia, 32,* 71–93.

Chomsky, C. (1979). Approaching reading through invented spelling. In L. Resnick & P. Weaver (Eds.), *Theory and practice of early reading* (Vol. 2, pp. 43–65). Hillsdale, NJ: Erlbaum.

Clay, M. (1991a). *Becoming literate: The construction of inner control.* Auckland, NZ: Heinemann.

Clay, M. (1991b). Introducing a new storybook to young readers. *Reading Teacher, 45,* 264–273.

Cramer, R. (2001). *Creative power: The nature and nurture of children's writing.* New York: Longman.

Fountas, I., & Pinnell, G. (1996). *Guided reading: Good first teaching for all children.* Portsmouth, NH: Heinemann.

Fraatz, J. M. (1987). *The politics of reading.* New York: Teachers College Press.

Gates, A. (1969). The tides of time. In J. Figurel (Ed.), *Reading and Realism* (pp. 12–20). Newark, DE: International Reading Association.

Graves, D. (1983). *Writing: Teachers and children at work.* Exeter, NH: Heinemann.

Gray, W.S. (1960). *On their own in reading.* Glenview, IL: Scott, Foresman.

Henderson, E. H. (1990). *Teaching spelling* (2nd ed.). Boston: Houghton Mifflin.

Hiebert, E. (1983). An examination of ability grouping for reading instruction. *Reading Research Quarterly, 18,* 231–255.

Hoffman, J. (1987). Rethinking the role of oral reading in basal instruction. *Elementary School Journal, 87,* 367–374.

Hoffman, J., McCarthey, S., Abbott, J., Christian, C., Corman, L., Curry, C., Dressman, M., Elliot, B., Matherne, D., & Stahle, D. (1994). So what's new in the new basals? A focus on first grade. *Journal of Reading Behavior, 26,* 47–73.

Invernizzi, M., Abouzeid, M., & Gill, J. T. (1994). Using students' invented spellings as a guide for spelling instruction that emphasizes word study. *Elementary School Journal, 95,* 155–167.

James, W. (1899). *Talks to teachers on psychology and to students on some of life's ideals.* Reprinted, New York: Dover Books, 1962.

Johnston, F. (2000). Word learning in predictable text. *Journal of Educational Psychology, 92,* 248–255.

Juel, C. (1988). Learning to read and write: A longitudinal study of 54 children from first through fourth grade. *Journal of Educational Psychology, 80,* 437–447.

Lyon, G. R. (1998). *Research on reading acquisition and reading disability.* Paper presented to the North Carolina Chapter of the International Dyslexia Association, Boone, NC.

Morris, D. (1993). The relationship between children's concept of word in text and phoneme awareness in learning to read: A longitudinal study. *Research in the Teaching of English, 27,* 133–154

Morris, D. (1999). *The Howard Street tutoring manual: Teaching at-risk readers in the primary grades.* New York: Guilford.

Morris, D., & Nelson, L. (1992). Supported oral reading with low-achieving second graders. *Reading Research and Instruction, 32,* 49–63.

Morris, D., & Perney, J. (1984). Developmental spelling as a predictor of first-grade reading achievement. *Elementary School Journal, 84,* 441–457.

Morris, D., Tyner, B., & Perney, J. (2000). Early Steps: Replicating the effects of a first-grade reading intervention program. *Journal of Educational Psychology, 92,* 681–693.

Pappas, C. (1991). Fostering full access to literacy by including information books. *Language Arts, 68,* 449–462.

Perfetti, C. (1985). *Reading ability.* New York: Oxford University Press.

Pinnell, G., Lyons, C., Deford, D., Bryk, A., & Seltzer, M. (1994). Comparing instructional models for the literacy education of high-risk first graders. *Reading Research Quarterly, 29,* 8–39.

Santa, C., & Hoien, T. (1999). An assessment of Early Steps: A program for early intervention of reading problems. *Reading Research Quarterly, 34,* 54–79.

Slavin, R. (1987). Ability grouping: A best-evidence synthesis. *Review of Educational Research, 57,* 293–336.

Slavin, R., Madden, N., Karweit, N., Dolan, L., & Wasik, B. (1994). Success for All: Getting reading right the first time. In E. Hiebert & B. Taylor (Eds.), *Getting reading right from the start* (pp. 125–147). Boston: Allyn & Bacon.

Snow, C., Burns, S., & Griffin, P. (1998). *Preventing reading difficulties in young children.* Washington, DC: National Academy Press.

Stanovich, K. (1986). Matthew effects in reading: Some consequences of individual differences in the acquisition of literacy. *Reading Research Quarterly, 21,* 360–406.

Stanovich, K. (1998). Twenty-five years of research on the reading process: The Grand Synthesis and what it means to our field. In T. Shanahan & F. Rodriguez-Brown (Eds.), *47th yearbook of the National Reading Conference* (pp. 44–58). Chicago: National Reading Conference.

Stauffer, R. (1970). *The language-experience approach to the teaching of reading.* New York: Harper & Row.

Temple, C., Nathan, R., Temple, F., & Burris, N. (1993). *The beginnings of writing* (3rd ed.). Boston: Allyn & Bacon.

Templeton, S. (1997). *Teaching the integrated language arts.* Boston: Houghton Mifflin.

Tharp, R., & Gallimore, R. (1988). *Rousing minds to life: Teaching, learning, and schooling in social context.* New York: Cambridge University Press.

Wells, G. (1986). *The meaning makers.* Portsmouth, NH: Heinemann.

Appendix

1. *Word-recognition task*

1. cat	11. bird	21. leg	31. table
2. is	12. saw	22. black	32. stand
3. like	13. feet	23. smile	33. gate
4. old	14. lake	24. dark	34. spill
5. your	15. hid	25. couldn't	35. pull
6. said	16. about	26. because	36. prize
7. big	17. rain	27. shout	37. shoot
8. not	18. how	28. glass	38. wrote
9. back	19. window	29. paint	39. able
10. sun	20. mother	30. children	40. change

2. *Spelling task*

Word	*Scores for sample spellings (correct spelling = 5 points)*			
	1 point	*2 points*	*3 points*	*4 points*
1. Back	b	bk, bc, ba	bak, back, bake	backe
2. Feet	f	ft, fe	fet	fete, feat
3. Step	s, c	sp, se, sa, st, stp	sap, cap, stap, sep	stepe
4. Junk	j, g	jk, gc, jo, gu	jok, juk, gok, gonk	gunk, junc, junck
5. Picking	p	pk, pc, pen, pek, pcn	pekn, pekin, peking	piking, picing
6. Mail	m	ml, ma	mal, mall, mel	male, malle
7. Side	s, c	sd, cd, si	sid, sod	sied, siad
8. Chin	c, g, j, h	cn, hn, ci, ce	cin, gen, hen, chen	chine, chinn
9. Dress	d, j, g	ds, js, ja, drs, drs	dras, jras, das, gas	dres, drese
10. Peeked	p	pk, pc, pt, pkt, pe	pekt, pect, pekd	peked, peaked
11. Lamp	l	lp, la	lap, lape, lam	lampe
12. Road	r	rd, ro	rod	rode, roed
13. Plant	p	pt, pa	pat, plat, plate	plante
14. Short	s	st, sot, sht	shot, sorte, sort	shorte
15. Grabbed	g	gb, gab, grad	gabd, grabd	grabed

Note: For a fuller explanation of the developmental spelling scoring system, see Morris & Perney (1984) or Morris, Tyner, & Perney (1999).

3. *Passage reading task*

Passage-reading level	Book exerpts*	Number of words	Accuracy criterion (%)
1. Emergent	*The Storm* (Cowley, 1983; entire book)	29	85
2. Preprimer	*Look for Me* (Melser, 1982; entire book)	69	85
3. Primer	*Mouse Tales* (Lobel, 1972; pp. 18–23)	100	90
4. Late first grade	*Frog and Toad All Year* (Lobel, 1976; pp. 30–33)	100	90
5. Early second grade	*Wild, Wild Wolves* (Milton, 1992; pp. 15–16)	100	92
6. Late second grade	*Kate Shelley and the Midnight Express* (Wetterer, 1990, pp. 6–8)	100	92

*The child reads each passage directly from the book.

4

Tutoring At-Risk Beginning Readers

Darrell Morris

In a typical first- or second-grade classroom, with a 1:24 teacher–student ratio and only ninety minutes of reading instruction, there is surprisingly little time available for individual children to read aloud under the classroom teacher's direct supervision. This lack of supervised reading time—a long-standing, systemic problem in elementary schools—is particularly harmful to low-achieving readers who desperately need practice in a situation where feedback is available. Like most of us facing a new and difficult task, the struggling beginning reader requires help when trouble arises (e.g., an unknown word) and reassurance when things are going well.

One powerful way to provide low-achieving readers with needed practice and feedback is to tutor them. Recently, several intervention programs, including Reading Recovery (Pinnell, Lyons, Deford, Bryk, & Seltzer, 1994), Success for All (Slavin et al., 1996), Early Steps (Santa & Hoien, 1999), and Howard Street (Morris, 1999a) have demonstrated that one-to-one tutoring can significantly raise the achievement of at-risk beginning readers. In truth, these tutoring programs have "opened the reading field's eyes," showing that at-risk children *can* learn to read—can catch up with their peers—if provided with sensible and intensive one-to-one instruction. In this chapter, I discuss the need for reading tutoring in the primary grades, provide a rationale for why tutoring works, and overview several research-tested tutoring models. I conclude by considering how an elementary school might mount an effective tutoring program for low-reading students in grades one, two, and three.

The Need for Tutoring

Low-reading primary-grade students are in a race against time. No matter how slow their start, they need to be reading at or near grade level by the end of third grade if they are to handle the reading demands of the mid-elementary curriculum. There have always been children who get off to a slow start in learning to read. To help them, American schools for many years have used small-group remedial or "pull-out" instruction beginning in second or third grade, and usually funded by Title I or Special Education (Slavin, 1991). Unfortunately, providing supplemental reading assistance *after* the students have fallen behind does not solve the problem. The low-reading second and third graders often improve their reading but they rarely catch up; they do not achieve the grade-level reading skill that is necessary for future academic success.

In the late 1970s, Marie Clay, a New Zealand developmental psychologist, directly challenged American assumptions about remedial reading instruction. Clay (1979) argued forcefully that effective "catch up" instruction would have to *begin earlier* (in first grade, when the child had not fallen too far behind) and be *more intensive* (one-to-one as opposed to small-group). In Figure 4.1, the ascending vertical arrows (↑) illustrate the logic behind Clay's "begin earlier" argument. It is true that first graders differ in reading readiness on school entry (see high, middle, and low readiness groups in the figure). However, across time, classroom reading instruction in first and second grade serves to widen these achievement differences. If the goal is to help low readers catch up with their average-achieving peers, why wait till the end of first or second grade (when the achievement gap has widened) to provide assistance? Instead, intervene at the beginning of first grade, when the achievement gap is smallest.

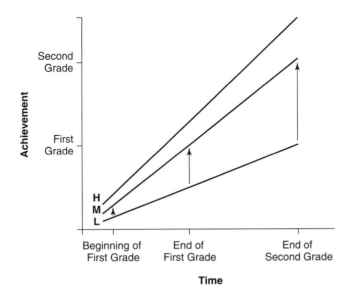

FIGURE 4.1 *Achievement trajectories of high (H), middle (M), and low (L) readiness readers across first and second grade*

Regarding how to intervene, Clay advocated intensive one-to-one, as opposed to small-group, reading instruction. She understood that, as classroom reading instruction commences in first grade, the average group does not stop and beckon the low group to hurry and catch up. Instead, the average readers progress at a rate that their aptitude or readiness allows. This puts the low readers in a seemingly untenable situation. To catch up with the average group, the low group *has to progress at a faster rate than the children who started out ahead of them.* Only daily, one-to-one instruction, Clay believed, could help low-readiness readers meet this formidable challenge.

However strong the case for tutorial intervention, at-risk readers also need effective classroom reading instruction if they are to achieve grade-level reading status by the end of third grade. Conceptually speaking, there are two hills that need to be climbed. First, we want low readers to catch up with their average-achieving peers; both quality classroom instruction for low readers and supplemental tutoring can help in this regard. Second, we want to make sure that the average-achieving or "middle" reading group in the classroom is working at a grade-level pace; that is, that they read at a late first-grade level at the end of first grade, at a late second-grade level at the end of second grade, and so on. Remember that the classroom teacher determines the pace of instruction for different reading groups (see Chapter 3, p. 49). In the long run, it does little good to help low readers catch up with the "middle of the class" if the middle is functioning well below grade level in reading.

Helping at-risk first graders achieve grade-level reading status is a considerable task, one that is often difficult to accomplish in just one school year. For this reason, many schools will need to think in terms of a two-year reading intervention plan (i.e., first *and* second grade). Supplemental tutoring in first grade can help low readers reach a critical or "launching pad" reading level (e.g., primer level). Then, follow-up tutoring in second grade (possibly not as intensive) can help the children advance to grade-level reading status by the end of the school year (see Morris, 2001). Figure 4.2 illustrates how such a two-year intervention might impact the "catch up" achievement of a group of low readers.

Why Tutoring Works

Anyone who has ever taken *group* lessons in tennis, golf, or ice skating at a local recreation center can appreciate the power of individual instruction. No matter how talented the instructor, in group lessons the best he or she can do is model the athletic behavior and then let the participants try it on their own. Given the group context, there is limited time for the instructor to provide learners with immediate feedback geared to their individual needs.

The opposite is true in individual lessons. For example, a skillful golf pro, when working with only one student, can zero in on that student's grip of the club, stance, and golf swing. Moreover, instead of speaking in generalities about proper grip, stance, and swing (information that can be found in any golf manual), the pro can take into consideration the idiosyncratic nature of the individual student's golf game, providing feedback and advice that may apply to the student's game (e.g.,

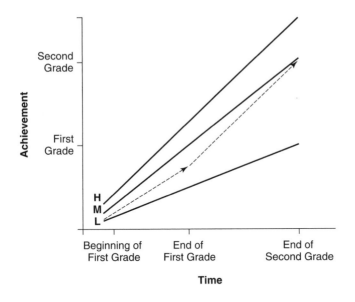

FIGURE 4.2 *Impact of a two-year tutorial intervention (see dotted line) on the reading achievement of low-readiness children*

"Slow down and shorten your backswing"), but not to that of another beginning golfer. Is it any wonder that when people of means seek such athletic instruction they opt for individual, not group, lessons?

For many children, learning to read is much more complex than learning to hit a golf ball. There is considerable failure when children are taught to read in groups, and, not surprisingly, instruction tailored to the needs of the individual child has proven to be more effective. In fact, today more than ever before, researchers and practitioners are beginning to appreciate the power of one-to-one tutoring in preventing reading failure in the primary grades (Invernizzi, Rosemary, Juel, & Richards, 1997; Pinnell et al., 1994; Santa & Hoien, 1999).

In explaining the potential of a one-to-one instructional setting, Wasik and Slavin (1990) argued that there are four components of effective instruction, which they called the QAIT model:

1. *Quality of instruction:* Skillfulness with which information or processes are presented so that they are easily learned by students. Quality of instruction involves what is taught and how it is presented;

2. *Appropriate level of instruction:* Ability to present lessons at the student's optimum learning level, that is, lessons that are neither too difficult nor too easy for the student;

3. *Incentive:* Timeliness in providing reinforcement and corrective feedback to the student in the act of learning;

4. *Time:* Provision of enough instructional and practice time so that the material or skill can be learned.

Wasik and Slavin stated that one-to-one tutoring can potentially affect all four components of the QAIT model. First, providing a tutor with careful training and good materials should ensure a reasonable *quality of instruction.* Second, a tutor can completely adapt the *level and pace of instruction* to the needs of the child being tutored. If the child requires additional instruction at a given level, this can be provided; if the child is "catching on," the tutor can quickly move forward. Wasik and Slavin correctly noted that such individualized pacing is not possible in "even one-to-two or one-to-three instruction, where adaptation to individual needs becomes progressively more difficult" (p. 6).

Third, a tutor can devote full attention to his or her student, providing *feedback or incentive* at exactly the moment it is called for in the learning process. Such timely feedback, whether it be praise or correction, enhances learning and increases student motivation. Fourth, if tutoring is provided as a supplement to classroom instruction, it adds to *instructional time.*

To Wasik and Slavin's four components of effective tutorial instruction I wish to add a fifth. It pertains to the *interpersonal bond* that often develops between tutor and child, a bond of mutual caring and trust that can nurture learning. The following excerpt from a detailed account of an after-school volunteer tutoring program (Morris, 1993) indicates the power of this tutor-child bond:

> We discovered quickly that in our program we needed mature tutors, college age or older. It takes a certain level of maturity or commitment to give up two afternoons per week for an entire year to tutor a child. Also, some of the children at times brought frustration and anxiety with them to the after-school tutoring lessons, creating management challenges for even a mature tutor.
>
> The flip-side of occasional misbehavior or recalcitrance was the inevitable bond that formed between the tutor and his/her child. The children in our program were not used to receiving a lot of individual attention in school, where class size ranged from 28 to 34. Initially, some of them would actually withdraw from the intimacy of the tutorial relationship, seeming to disbelieve or distrust it. For example, Quincy, a street-wise third grader with a strong aversion to the printed word, alternated between shyness and surliness in the fall. I clearly remember Quincy's words to his tutor around Christmas of that year, 'When you gonna leave, Warn?' At first, Warren did not understand the question, but then he answered, 'I'm not leaving, Quincy, I'm gonna be here all year long.' From that point on, Quincy 'opened up,' both in his personal relationship with his tutor and in his willingness to take risks in reading and writing. Quincy learned to read that year . . . (pp. 68–69).

It should come as no surprise that consistent, one-to-one instruction provided by a knowledgeable, caring adult can help an at-risk child learn how to read. But how does one conceptualize a tutoring program for struggling beginning readers?

For example, which group of children should be tutored (first, second, or third graders)? Who should do the tutoring (teachers, paraprofessionals, or volunteers) and what training should the tutors receive? What instructional methods and materials should be used? How frequently should the tutoring lessons occur (two, three, five days per week)? Finally, how does one determine if a tutoring program is making an educational difference? We turn now to research-based tutoring models that have addressed these very questions.

Research-Based Tutorial Models

In this section, I review two programs (Reading Recovery and Early Steps) that use certified teachers to tutor at-risk readers and two programs (Howard Street and Book Buddies) that use community volunteers to tutor.

Reading Recovery

Reading Recovery, a prevention-oriented tutoring program originally developed in New Zealand in the late 1970s (Clay, 1979, 1993), has been used widely in the United States for the past fifteen years (Pinnell, 1989; Smith-Burke, 2001). In this program, at-risk readers are identified at the beginning of first grade using a diagnostic survey. The students are then tutored thirty minutes per day, five days per week by a carefully trained teacher. The students receive from sixty to eighty tutoring lessons, whereupon they are labeled *discontinued* (having successfully reached the "middle of the class" in reading) or *not discontinued* (having not reached the "middle of the class" criterion). In either case, the children leave the program at midyear, and a second group of low-reading first graders begins to receive the Reading Recovery tutoring.

The Reading Recovery lesson plan (thirty minutes) is elegant in design and based on the premise that neophyte readers learn best when they engage in reading and writing meaningful texts. The daily lesson consists of three parts:

1. *Rereading familiar books.* The child rereads three short, natural-language books, with the tutor offering support as needed. During the reading, the tutor encourages the child to use strategies (e.g., multiple cue use [beginning letter, sentence, and picture] for word identification, self-correction, prediction, etc.) that will eventually lead to self-control of the reading process.

2. *Sentence writing.* Each day the child writes a sentence of his or her own choice. At the beginning of the year, the tutor supports the child in "hearing" sounds in words and forming letters. As the child improves in these areas, the tutor lessens the amount of assistance provided. In this part of the lesson, the tutor may also stop and teach a given letter-sound, sight word, or spelling pattern that is giving the child problems.

3. *Introduction of a new book.* The tutor and child preview the new book, identifying difficult vocabulary, and surveying the pictures in order to predict the story line.

Then the child returns to page one and attempts to read the new story, the tutor providing assistance as needed. The new book is then reread in Part 1 of the next day's lesson.

Although the lesson plan remains constant, each child's program differs. On a daily basis, the tutor selects specific books to meet the needs of an individual child, and the child chooses the message he or she wishes to write. "The major difference within and across [Reading Recovery] lessons lies in the teacher's ability to follow each child and to respond in ways that support acceleration and the development of strategies" (Wasik & Slavin, 1993, p. 184).

Because success in Reading Recovery depends so much on the individual tutor's judgment and decision making, tutors receive very careful guidance during their training year. Each week throughout the year, eight to ten tutors (usually reading teachers) gather with an expert trainer behind a one-way glass to observe "live" Reading Recovery lessons and discuss the theory and practice of tutoring struggling readers. Then the teachers go back to their respective schools and apply the training by tutoring up to four different children on a daily basis. This intensive, yearlong clinical training for teachers is a hallmark of the Reading Recovery program.

At the end of the first-grade year, Reading Recovery students are routinely tested on informal word-recognition and passage-reading tasks. Results in several studies have shown that groups of students receiving Reading Recovery instruction consistently outperform closely matched comparison groups, and that approximately two-thirds of the tutored children achieve the "middle-of-the-class" reading criterion (Center, Wheldall, Freeman, Outhread, & McNaught, 1995; DeFord, Pinnell, Lyons, & Young, 1988; Shanahan & Barr, 1995).

The major strengths of Reading Recovery are its proven ability to raise the achievement of at-risk first-grade readers and its intensive, yearlong practicum training for participating teachers. Criticisms of the program pertain to (1) expense—both the cost of training and the cost of one-to-one tutoring by certified teachers; (2) the limited number of students one Reading Recovery teacher can serve in an elementary school; (3) questions about the maintenance of Reading Recovery achievement gains in succeeding years; and (4) the program's lack of a systematic phonics component that might better meet the needs of a certain group of at-risk first-grade readers. (See Shanahan & Barr, 1995, for a comprehensive review of Reading Recovery.)

Early Steps

Early Steps, a first-grade tutorial intervention, is similar to Reading Recovery in philosophy and design. Like the more established program, Early Steps emphasizes early identification of at-risk readers; intensive one-to-one tutoring on a daily basis; and careful, yearlong teacher training (Morris, Tyner, & Perney, 2000). Early Steps even uses a daily lesson plan that is similar in format to Reading Recovery's. Nonetheless, there are important differences between the two intervention programs, particularly regarding word-study instruction and method of teacher training.

Early Steps, unlike Reading Recovery, includes a systematic word-study component in the thirty-minute lesson:

1. Rereading familiar books (10 min.)
2. Word study (7 min.)
3. Sentence writing (7 min.)
4. Introduction of a new book (6 min.)

One-fourth of each tutoring lesson is devoted to helping the child learn basic letter–sound relationships and spelling patterns (e.g., beginning consonants, short-vowel word families, short- and long-vowel patterns). The word study is developmentally paced to the needs of the individual child, and the emphasis is on mastery or internalization of the patterns taught (see *Teaching word recognition:* Chapter 3, p. 44).

Regarding tutor training, in Early Steps a school must be willing to train not just its reading teacher (as is often the case in Reading Recovery), but also its first-grade classroom teachers. This means that a "team" of teachers within a given school goes through the training year together. There are fewer training sessions in Early Steps (ten sessions as opposed to thirty sessions in Reading Recovery), and the nature of the tutoring training is a bit different. While both programs train tutors how to pace low readers efficiently through a graded set of reading materials, Early Steps training places more emphasis on systematic phonics instruction and less on explicit strategy instruction.

In two yearlong studies (Morris et al., 2000; Santa & Hoien, 1999), Early Steps-tutored children outperformed comparison groups on both informal and standardized measures of first-grade reading achievement. In both studies, two thirds of the tutored children reached the primer reading level or higher and, interestingly, Early Steps tutoring made the largest difference for those children who were most at risk (lowest in reading ability) in September.

Like Reading Recovery, Early Steps raises the achievement of at-risk first-grade readers while providing valuable pedagogical training to participating teachers. In addition, because of the way the training is structured, Early Steps leaves behind in a given school a "team" of classroom and specialist teachers who share the same knowledge base, set of experiences, and language. On the downside, a limited number of students can be served if full-time teachers do the tutoring, and there is not yet evidence that Early Steps reading gains in first grade are maintained in later grades. Also, whereas Reading Recovery has established a nationwide, university-based infrastructure for training teachers, Early Steps is limited to perhaps a dozen itinerant trainers scattered throughout the United States.

The Howard Street Tutoring Program

The Howard Street Tutoring Program shares parenting with Early Steps, but differs from it and from other interventions in two major ways. First, the program was originally designed for low-reading second and third graders (as opposed to first graders), and second, it uses volunteers instead of certified teachers to tutor children (Morris, 1999a, 2001).

In the Howard Street model, a group of eight to twelve community volunteers (parents, college students, business employees, senior citizens, etc.) come to an elementary school at the same time two days per week (e.g., from 1:00 to 1:45 P.M. on Mondays and Wednesdays). Each volunteer tutors one second or third grader using a lesson plan that has been prepared by a reading specialist supervisor. The lesson contains four parts:

1. *Guided reading at the child's instructional level* (twenty minutes). The child, with the tutor's support, reads aloud a well-written basal story or tradebook.

2. *Word study* (ten minutes). The child practices sorting, reading, and spelling the various one-syllable vowel patterns (CVC, CVCe, CVVC, and CV-r).

3. *Easy reading* (ten minutes). To develop fluency and confidence, the child rereads a familiar story or partner-reads with the tutor a new, but easy, book.

4. *Reading to the child* (five minutes). If time allows, the tutor reads to the child a fairy tale, fable, picture book, or chapter from a longer book.

As the volunteers carry out the lesson plan, the supervisor walks around the room, providing encouragement and feedback as needed.

The supervisor's lesson planning ensures quality control in the program. Through the lesson plans, the supervisor is able to differentiate skill instruction (beginning consonants for one child, short-vowel word families for another) and adjust the pace at which individual children progress through the graded reading materials (primer, late first, early second, and so on). Such instructional "fine-tuning" increases student achievement, but does come at a cost. That is, the supervisor of ten tutor–child pairs must spend approximately two hours of planning per tutoring day in the fall and up to one and a half hours per tutoring day during the spring.

Preplanned lessons for the individual children are crucial, yet equally important is the supervisor's physical presence *during* the tutoring period. As the supervisor walks among and observes the ten tutor–child pairs, he or she sends an implicit message to child and volunteer alike: "This tutoring is important business." During a lesson, the supervisor can model a new teaching technique for a tutor or provide assistance when an old technique does not seem to be working. Moreover, the supervisor's firsthand observations of the tutoring enable him or her to make informed and necessary adjustments in upcoming lessons (e.g., to move a child up one reading level or one skill level).

A typical Howard Street tutoring lesson might unfold as follows. Mrs. Turner, a volunteer tutor, arrives at school at 8:25 on a Monday morning and picks up her tutoring materials (books, word cards, and lesson-plan notebook). She quickly glances at today's lesson plan, which has been written out by the reading teacher, Ms. Summers:

> ***Guided Reading:*** Read "Robber in the Woods," the next story in *Toothless Dragon* (a 1-2 basal reader with controlled vocabulary).
>
> ***Word Study:*** Sort *a* patterns: *hat, make,* and *card.* Play memory game.
>
> ***Easy Reading:*** Partner-read *Danny and the Dinosaur* (a primer-level tradebook).
>
> ***Read To:*** Read *Wiley and the Hairy Man* (an African folktale).

Vincent, Mrs. Turner's second-grade tutee, bounds into the reading room at 8:30 A.M., and the two quickly get down to work.

After previewing or looking at the pictures in the first six pages of "Robber in the Woods," Mrs. Turner asks Vincent to predict who the robber might be. He responds that "it's a guy who broke out of jail and is looking to steal a car." "That's an interesting prediction," says Mrs. Turner, "let's go back and read the story." The tutor and child alternate reading aloud the first four pages and then stop for a comprehension check. Because Vincent is reading well, the tutor allows him to read the next eight pages independently, stopping him now and then to discuss the characters and plot. They end the reading at an interesting point (Vincent now thinks the "robber" is a grizzly bear who is looking for food), and will finish the story during the next tutoring lesson.

The word-sort activity goes well, with Vincent easily sorting and reading the *a*-pattern words (he has been working on these three patterns for two weeks).

hat	*make*	*park*
mad	page	card
ran	late	jar
clap	name	start
flag	trade	farm

Next, Vincent and the tutor play Memory, a game in which the same word cards are mixed and then placed face down on the table.

A player turns over two cards, looking for a pattern match (e.g., *make* and *name*). If he or she obtains a match (and can read the words), he or she removes the two words from the table and takes another turn. The game ends when all of the words are removed from the table. Vincent loves to play Memory, and today his ability to read the words accurately and immediately tells Mrs. Turner that it is time to increase the difficulty of the word-sorting task.

During the easy reading or reading-for-fluency part of the lesson, Vincent and the tutor partner-read *Danny and the Dinosaur*. Vincent reads aloud four consecutive pages and then Mrs. Turner reads four pages. In this partner-reading format, they are able to complete the tradebook in about twelve minutes.

Mrs. Turner ends the forty-five-minute lesson by reading to Vincent the first half of *Wiley and the Hairy Man*. The child is engrossed in this folktale, a story worthy of his imagination.

During Vincent's lesson, six other tutor–child pairs were working simultaneously either in the same or an adjacent room. Ms. Summers, the reading teacher, continually circulated through the rooms, observing parts of each child's lesson. For example, she saw parts of Vincent's guided reading and word study. Based on her observations—and notes that Vincent's tutor quickly jotted down at the end of the lesson—Ms. Summers plans the following tutoring lesson for Vincent on Wednesday.

> *Guided Reading:* Read second half of "Robber in the Woods" in *Toothless Dragon* (1-2 basal).
>
> *Word Study:* Sort *a*-patterns: *hat, make, park,* and *rain* (note new *ai* pattern).
>
> *Easy Reading:* Partner-read *All Stuck Up*, a primer-level version of Brer Rabbit and the Tarbaby.
>
> *Read To:* Read second half of *Wiley and the Hairy Man*.

We can see from Ms. Summers's Monday and Wednesday lesson plans for Vincent that the tutoring lessons are not completely separate entities, but instead build on one another—an interesting mixture of the *old* (which provides continuity and needed review) and the *new* (which provides interest and challenge).

In a careful evaluation of the Howard Street Tutoring Program, Morris, Shaw, and Perney (1990) found that a group of thirty tutored children outperformed a closely-matched comparison group on several reading and spelling measures. Over an eight-month period, the average gain in contextual reading for the tutored group was 12.2 months while the average gain for the comparison group was only 6.6 months. This is one of the few studies that has tested the effectiveness of using volunteers to tutor low readers (see Wasik, 1998).

The obvious advantage of the Howard Street volunteer tutoring model is its low cost. Morris (2001) estimated that it costs 8 times as much to serve a student with a Reading Recovery tutor as it does to serve a student with a supervised volunteer tutor. Thus, volunteer tutoring programs can potentially serve many more low-reading children than can professionally staffed tutoring programs. Of course, professional expertise is required in the Howard Street model. For the program to work, a school needs a knowledgeable reading teacher who is committed to spending time and energy in supervising volunteer tutors. Most reading teachers would require some training in order to implement the Howard Street tutoring model; still, this *supervisor* training would be shorter in duration and less intensive than the teacher training found in either Reading Recovery or Early Steps.

Book Buddies

The Book Buddies tutoring program in Charlottesville, Virginia, is the first large-scale attempt to use community volunteers to tutor at-risk beginning readers. The program serves approximately 150 children per year in six elementary schools (Invernizzi, 2001).

Book Buddies is a creative hybrid of the Howard Street and Reading Recovery tutoring models. The program focuses on at-risk first-grade readers (Reading Recovery); it uses volunteer tutors who are closely supervised by a reading specialist two days per week (Howard Street); and it employs a four-part, forty-five-minute lesson plan that combines aspects of both the Reading Recovery and Howard Street lesson plans; for example:

1. *Easy reading.* The child rereads familiar books to develop fluency and confidence.
2. *Word study.* The child works on alphabet and phonics concepts.
3. *Writing for sounds.* The child attempts to write a teacher-dictated sentence, concentrating on the individual sounds within the words.
4. *Reading a new book.* With the tutor's help, the child reads aloud a new book.

As the child progresses to a late-preprimer reading level, the Book Buddies lesson plan is slightly modified to include more emphasis on comprehension and independent writing.

As with the Howard Street program, the "hub" around which Book Buddies revolves is the supervisor or "coordinator" of tutoring. The coordinator, a masters-level reading specialist, writes lesson plans, arranges the materials for each lesson, and supplies routine feedback to the volunteer tutors regarding teaching technique and pacing (Invernizzi, 2001). Although the coordinators were originally funded by a soft-money grant, the success of Book Buddies eventually led the local school district to assume responsibility for the coordinators' half-time salaries. The school district also employs a half-time person to recruit the large number of volunteer tutors who are needed each year.

In a formal evaluation of the first three cohorts of the Charlottesville Book Buddies program, results showed large effect sizes for the tutored group, particularly in the area of word recognition. In addition, the program's effectiveness improved each successive year (Invernizzi, Rosemary, Juel, & Richards, 1997). In a follow-up study, Book Buddies was implemented in a poor neighborhood school in the South Bronx (New York), with Americorps and VISTA workers serving as volunteer tutors. Results showed that two cohorts of Book Buddies first graders, each receiving one-half year of tutoring, significantly outperformed comparison groups on a variety of reading measures (Meier & Invernizzi, in press).

Again, cost-effectiveness is a major advantage of the Book Buddies volunteer tutoring program. Even when program coordinators are a paid a half-time salary by the school district, the cost of the tutoring is less than $1,000 per child, or one fourth the cost of a professionally staffed tutoring program like Reading Recovery. Like Howard Street, Book Buddies must eventually tackle the problem of "upscaling," that is, how to train a large number of reading teachers across the country to implement the program successfully in their own communities. Morris (2001) stated:

> It is one thing for a few college reading professors and their students (e.g., Invernizzi et al., 1997; Morris et al., 1990) to show that a group of closely supervised volunteers can significantly raise the achievement of at-risk readers. It is quite another to show that this phenomenon can be replicated by reading teachers in schools across the country (pp. 188–189).

The issue of upscaling notwithstanding, the Charlottesville Book Buddies program has made an important contribution. The program serves as a model for how a school system, working closely with a local university, can meaningfully involve the community in helping at-risk children learn to read.

Summary Comments

Three of the four interventions described above focus on first grade. In this sense, the programs are following Marie Clay's advice to intervene early, before at-risk children fall significantly behind in reading. Still, one of the interventions (Howard Street) provides tutoring to low-reading second and third graders, and another (Book Buddies) is presently being modified to do the same (see Invernizzi, 2001). It seems that reading educators are starting to realize that, while intervening in first grade is crucially important, follow-up tutorial help in second and third grade will be needed by many low-reading children.

A second commonality is that all four tutoring programs feature a balanced instructional routine. Reading for meaning is emphasized, but word study and writing also play important parts in the lesson plan. In fact, three of the four programs (all except Reading Recovery) include a systematic phonics component to help at-risk readers improve their word recognition and spelling ability.

Finally, teacher expertise is integral to the success of each of the interventions. Reading Recovery and Early Steps help teachers develop specialized pedagogical knowledge through intensive, yearlong clinical training. Using a learning-through-doing or practicum approach (see Morris, 1999b; Schon, 1987), these programs deepen teachers' understanding of the learning-to-read process and improve their ability to use various methods and materials in timely and appropriate ways. Their positive effects on children's learning notwithstanding, Reading Recovery and Early Steps might best be thought of as exemplary teacher-development models.

The Howard Street and Book Buddies programs also require teacher expertise, in this case a knowledgeable reading specialist to carefully supervise the work of volunteer tutors. Without expert supervision, these volunteer-staffed programs would not be viable.

A School-Based Plan for Tutoring At-Risk Beginning Readers

In the preceding section I established that successful reading tutorials include the following ingredients: early intervention (with follow-up as needed), balanced instruction, and teacher expertise. In this section, I describe how these ingredients can be combined in a comprehensive school-based plan to provide quality tutoring to at-risk, primary-grade readers.

The Paradox of Tutorial Intervention

Professionally staffed tutorial interventions such as Reading Recovery and Early Steps present a paradox to schools. The interventions work—they raise children's reading achievement—but they are so expensive that many schools can provide such tutoring to only a small number of the children who need it. For example, Shanahan and Barr (1995) estimated the cost of Reading Recovery tutoring to be $4,000 per child. Consider a poor rural or urban school with twenty-four at-risk readers spread across three first-grade classrooms. If we multiply 24 × $4,000, we find that it will cost $96,000 or the equivalent of two to three full-time teachers to provide pull-out tutoring to each first-grade child. Over the long run, this is an expense that most school districts in the United States will not be able to bear.

If one-to-one tutoring by carefully trained teachers is cost-prohibitive in schools serving large numbers of at-risk children (but see Success for All, Chapter 5), then what are the alternatives? First, we can develop and refine effective small-group interventions for low-achieving readers. Much attention should be given to this task, because small-group instructional routines can be used in both the regular classroom and supplementary pull-out programs (see Hiebert, 1994; Hoffman, 1987; Morris & Nelson, 1992). Note, however, that it is difficult for small-group instruction, no matter how well planned or skillfully implemented, to compete with a tutorial. As Wasik and Slavin (1990) have argued, a one-to-one setting ensures that a child is taught consistently at the appropriate level, and is provided with timely reinforcement and corrective feedback during reading. Such individually paced instruction, on which catch-up or accelerated learning may depend, is not possible in a small-group context.

A second alternative is to spread tutoring opportunities more widely within a school by having paraprofessionals (teacher aides or paid part-time tutors) and community volunteers work with at-risk readers. The use of noncertified but competent adult tutors greatly reduces the cost of tutoring and, thus, increases the number of children who could be served. The question is this: Can paraprofessional and volunteer tutors deliver instruction that will make a real difference in the achievement of at-risk readers? I believe the answer is yes, but, ironically, the success of nonprofessional tutors depends directly on the professional expertise of a school-based reading teacher.

A New Role for the Reading Teacher

Traditionally, the dual role of the school reading teacher has been to provide instruction to small groups of low readers and to consult with classroom teachers regarding reading-related issues. I propose an expansion of this role. In addition to providing direct instruction to students and consultation to teachers, I suggest that the reading teacher begin to supervise paraprofessional and volunteer tutors as they provide one-to-one instruction to low readers. In this way, the reading teacher can "work through" other adults to extend and intensify the instruction offered to low readers.

Scheduling Reading Instruction. Figure 4.3 indicates the number of children who can be tutored within a school when a reading teacher opts to supervise para-professional and volunteer tutors. Figure 4.4 shows how the reading teacher might schedule his or her teaching/supervisory workload across the days of the week. Note in Figure 4.4 that on Monday through Friday the *reading teacher* tutors two first graders and teaches one first-grade "readiness" group (four children who lack basic alphabet and letter–sound knowledge). On Monday, Wednesday, and Friday, the reading teacher teaches two second-grade groups and on Tuesday and Thursday,

---

Reading Teacher
    Tutors 2 first graders (M–F: 30 minutes)   (22)
    Teaches a group of 4 first graders (M–F: 45 minutes)
    Teaches a group of 4 second graders (M, W, F: 45 minutes)
    Teaches a second group of 4 second graders (M, W, F: 45 minutes)
    Teaches a group of 4 third graders (T, Th: 45 minutes)

Teacher Aides
    2 first-grade aides each tutor 2 first-grade students (M–F: 30 minutes)   (4)
    2 second-grade aides each tutor 2 second-grade students
        (M–F: 30 minutes)   (4)

Volunteer Tutors
    8 volunteer tutors each tutor 1 second-grade student (T, TH: 45 minutes)   (8)
    6 volunteer tutors each tutor 1 third-grade student (M, W: 45 minutes)   (6)

                                              Total number of tutored students   (24)

FIGURE 4.3 *Number of children served when a reading teacher supervises paraprofessional and volunteer tutors*

| Time | Day of Week | | | | |
	Monday	Tuesday	Wednesday	Thursday	Friday
8:30	tutor 1st grade child				→
9:00	tutor another 1st grade child				→
9:30	BREAK				→
9:45	teach 2nd grade group (A)	teach 3rd grade group	teach 2nd grade group (A)	teach 3rd grade group	teach 2nd grade group (A)
10:30	teach 1st grade readiness group				→
11:00	LUNCH/PLANNING				→
12:00	supervise 4 tutor/child pairs (2 first graders and 2 second graders tutored by teacher aides)				→
12:30	supervise 4 tutor/child pairs (2 first graders and 2 second graders tutored by teacher aides)				→
1:00	BREAK				→
1:15	teach 2nd grade group (B)	supervise 8 tutor/child pairs (second graders tutored by volunteers	teach 2nd grade group (B)	supervise 8 tutor/child pairs (second graders tutored by volunteers	teach 2nd grade group (B)
2:00	supervise 6 tutor/child pairs (third graders tutored by volunteers	PLANNING	supervise 6 tutor/child pairs (third graders tutored by volunteers	PLANNING	PLANNING
2:45	End of day				

FIGURE 4.4 *Reading teacher's weekly schedule*

one third-grade group. The rest of the reading teacher's time is spent planning lessons and supervising the tutoring of teacher aides and community volunteers. Two *teacher aides* from first-grade classrooms each tutor two first graders Monday through Friday, and two teacher aides from second-grade classrooms tutor two second graders. These teacher aides tutor during the same one-hour period each day so that the reading teacher can observe them as a group. Finally, eight *community volunteers* come to the school at the same time on Tuesday and Thursday to tutor eight second graders. (The reading teacher plans these lessons and observes the tutoring.) Six more volunteers come to the school at the same time on Monday and Wednesday to tutor six third graders. (Again, the tutor plans the lessons and observes the tutoring.)

In the hypothetical schedule above, the reading teacher serves twenty-eight children spread across first, second, and third grade. Small-group instruction occurs each day, but what makes the schedule different is that, under the reading teacher's supervision, twenty-four of the twenty-eight children receive one-to-one instruction two or more times per week. Six first graders and four second graders receive 150 minutes of tutoring per week, while another eight second graders and six third graders receive ninety minutes of tutoring per week. Keep in mind that just ninety minutes of tutoring per week adds up to about fifty hours of one-to-one instruction over the course of a school year. This is the kind of intensive reading practice that Clay (1979) called for, and the kind that is found in the successful Howard Street and Book Buddies tutoring programs.

The Tutors.   To keep in practice and sharpen his or her skills, the reading teacher tutors two first-grade children each day. However, the remainder of the one-to-one tutoring is done by teacher aides and community volunteers (parents, college students, and retirees) under the close supervision of the reading teacher. Regarding the teacher aides, initially the reading teacher plans their lessons and monitors their tutoring on a daily basis. After a month or so, as the aides become familiar with the tutoring model, the reading teacher turns over to them some of the lesson planning responsibility and also begins to observe the aides' tutoring lessons on a less frequent basis (perhaps two times per week). Still, the reading teacher is available to the aides each day to answer questions, model instructional techniques, and help with pacing decisions (i.e., to decide if and when to move a child to a higher reading or word-study level).

The volunteer tutors, who come in only two times per week, require close, ongoing supervision. Volunteers are interested in helping children. They are not usually enthralled with the intricacies of phonics concepts or reading levels, nor do they wish to spend time planning reading lessons outside of the tutoring context. Nonetheless, if the reading teacher provides a well-planned lesson each tutoring day (e.g., specific books for the child to read, specific word patterns to sort and spell), volunteers can do a very effective job of teaching children to read.

If schools do not have teacher aides in the primary grades, an alternative source of tutors would be paraprofessionals or part-time tutors hired on an hourly basis. In just two and a half hours per day, the part-time tutor, working under supervision of a reading teacher, could tutor four low-reading children. An excellent and generally untapped source of volunteer tutors would be preservice teachers enrolled in a local university teacher-training program. There could be no finer experience for these teachers-in-training than to tutor a child in reading under the direct supervision of a specialist.

Training the Supervisor of Tutors. The tutoring plan outlined above will be effective only to the degree that the paraprofessional and volunteer tutors receive knowledgeable supervision from a school-based reading specialist. Unfortunately, how to initiate and supervise a quality tutoring program is not usually included in the professional training of reading teachers. To succeed, a reading teacher needs (1) a theoretical understanding of the learning-to-read process, (2) a practical model or plan for tutoring beginning readers, including materials, methods, and use of time, and (3) hands-on experience in using the tutoring model. Such knowledge is best acquired in a *practicum,* a training context in which a teacher can try out new ideas and procedures while receiving feedback on his or her performance from a *coach* or expert (Morris, 1999b; Schon, 1987). With regard to training tutor supervisors, several practicum possibilities come to mind.

First, the reading teacher could participate in a yearlong early intervention program such as Reading Recovery or Early Steps. By tutoring one or more at-risk beginning readers while receiving ongoing feedback from a trainer, the reading teacher would internalize a tutoring model (theoretical perspective, materials, teaching strategies) that he or she could later share with adult tutors under his or her supervision. Of course, the professional training would need to include information on how to modify the Reading Recovery or Early Steps tutoring procedures for use by paraprofessionals and community volunteers. In this case, the less complicated the professional training model, the easier it might be to modify for use by noncertified adult tutors.

A second way to prepare tutor supervisors is to have them participate in an intensive, three-week summer practicum. Morris (2001) suggested the following practicum format:

> Twelve reading teachers and a trainer would come together [for 3.5 hours each morning]. From 9:00 to 9:45 A.M., six of the teachers would each tutor [a child], and the other six teachers would observe. Then from 9:45 to 10:30 A.M., six new second graders would come in, and the teachers would reverse roles (the original tutors becoming observers, and vice versa). After an hour of lesson planning and individual conferencing with the trainer, the teachers would attend a closing one-hour seminar (11:30 A.M. to 12:30 P.M.). Here the trainer would lead discussions on teaching technique (guided reading and word study); would facilitate staffing of the tutored children; and, in the last few days of the practicum, would answer questions that the teachers might have about starting their own volunteer tutoring programs in the fall (p. 189).
>
> In such a summer practicum, participating reading teachers would learn through direct experience how to organize and implement a tutoring program. They would learn about reading materials and specific teaching techniques by using them daily, and *they would learn a method for supervising volunteer tutors through the experience of being supervised themselves* . . . (p. 189, italics added).

A third possibility for training tutor supervisors resides in colleges of education. Most master's-degree programs in reading education offer an on-campus reading practicum course similar to one described by Morris. Such a course could be modified and taken into the schools, on a contract basis, to teach reading teachers how to organize and implement tutoring programs in their schools.

A reading teacher who attempts to supervise a tutoring program will need commitment, interpersonal skills, and a good deal of energy. In addition, to be successful he or she will need specific, how-to-do-it knowledge, knowledge that is best developed in the practicum contexts described above.

Conclusion

In this chapter I have made a case for early reading intervention in the form of one-to-one tutoring. Programs like Reading Recovery, Early Steps, Howard Street, and Book Buddies have clearly shown the potential of such an approach. Tutoring is not a substitute for good classroom reading instruction in the primary grades (see Chapters 2 and 3). Rather, it is the combination of good classroom instruction plus tutoring that can help prevent reading failure for many at-risk children.

There are, of course, issues associated with tutoring. When certified teachers are used as reading tutors, the cost is high, prohibitively high for some school districts. When paraprofessionals or volunteers do the tutoring, the cost is reduced considerably but issues of training and supervision come to the fore. In fact, the effective use of volunteer tutors actually requires reading teachers to rethink and restructure the way they deliver instruction.

I believe that the potential benefits of tutoring justify wrestling with the issues of cost and supervision. In the century-long search for an answer to the problem of early reading failure, schools have invariably looked for packaged programs to deliver a quick solution. Unfortunately, good reading instruction cannot be packaged. It is true that appropriate materials are needed, but even more important are knowledgeable, problem-solving teachers and time (or opportuntity) for children to learn. I believe that the tutoring programs described in this chapter speak to the issues of teacher knowledge and student opportunity to learn. They address the careful training of individual teachers and the careful instruction of individual students. Far from being a quick fix, these programs represent thoughtful responses to a complex problem. For this reason, they deserve consideration.

References

Center, Y., Wheldall, K., Freeman, L., Outhred, L., & McNaught, M. (1995). An evaluation of Reading Recovery. *Reading Research Quarterly, 30,* 240–263.

Clay, M. (1979). *The early detection of reading difficulties.* Auckland, NZ: Heinemann.

Clay, M. (1993). *Reading Recovery: A guidebook for teachers in training.* Auckland, NZ: Heinemann.

Deford, D., Pinnell, G., Lyons, C., & Young, P. (1988). *Reading Recovery: Vol. 9. Report of the follow-up studies.* Columbus: Ohio State University.

Hiebert, E. (1994). A small-group literacy intervention with Chapter 1 students. In E. Hiebert & B. Taylor (Eds.), *Getting reading right from the start: Effective early literacy interventions* (pp. 85–106). Boston, MA: Allyn & Bacon.

Hoffman, J. (1987). Rethinking the role of oral reading in basal instruction. *Elementary School Journal, 87*, 367–374.

Invernizzi, M. (2001). Book Buddies: A community volunteer tutorial program. In L. Morrow & D. Woo (Eds.), *Tutoring programs for struggling readers: The America Reads Challenge* (pp. 193–215). New York: Guilford.

Invernizzi, M., Rosemary, C., Juel, C., & Richards, H. (1997). At-risk readers and community volunteers: A three-year perspective. *Journal of Scientific Studies of Reading, 1*, 277–300.

Meier, J., & Invernizzi, M. (in press). Book Buddies in the Bronx: Testing a model for America Reads and national service. *Journal of Education for Students Placed at Risk.*

Morris, D. (1993). *A selective history of the Howard Street Tutoring Program (1979–1989).* (ERIC Document Reproduction Service No. 355 473).

Morris, D. (1999a). *The Howard Street tutoring manual: Teaching at-risk readers in the primary grades.* New York: Guilford.

Morris, D. (1999b). The role of clinical training in the teaching of reading. In D. Evensen & P. Mosenthal (Eds.), *Advances in reading/language research: Vol. 6. Reconsidering the role of the reading clinic in a new age of literacy* (pp. 69–100). Stamford, CT: JAI Press.

Morris, D. (2001). The Howard Street tutoring model: Using volunteer tutors to prevent reading failure in the primary grades. In L. Morrow & D. Woo (Eds.), *Tutoring programs for struggling readers: The America Reads Challenge* (pp. 177–192). New York: Guilford.

Morris, D., & Nelson, L. (1992). Supported oral reading with low-achieving second graders. *Reading Research and Instruction, 32*, 49–63.

Morris, D., Shaw, B., & Perney, J. (1990). Helping low readers in grades two and three: An after-school volunteer tutoring program. *Elementary School Journal, 91*, 133–150.

Morris, D., Tyner, B., & Perney, J. (2000). Early Steps: Replicating the effects of a first-grade reading intervention program. *Journal of Educational Psychology, 92*, 681–693.

Pinnell, G. (1989). Reading Recovery: Helping at-risk children learn to read. *Elementary School Journal, 90*, 161–183.

Pinnell, G., Lyons, C., Deford, D., Bryk, A., & Seltzer, M. (1994). Comparing instructional models for the literacy education of high-risk first graders. *Reading Research Quarterly, 29*, 8–39.

Santa, C., & Hoien, T. (1999). An assessment of Early Steps: A program for early intervention of reading problems. *Reading Research Quarterly, 34*, 54–79.

Schon, D. (1987). *Educating the reflective practitioner.* San Francisco: Jossey-Bass.

Shanahan, T., & Barr, R. (1995). Reading Recovery: An independent evaluation of the effects of an early instructional intervention for at-risk learners. *Reading Research Quarterly, 30*, 958–996.

Slavin, R. (1991). Chapter 1: A vision for the next quarter century. *Phi Delta Kappan, 72*, 586–592.

Slavin, R., Madden, N., Dolan, L., Wasik, B., Ross, S., Smith, L., & Dianda, M. (1996). Success for All: A summary of the research. *Journal of Education for Students Placed at Risk, 1*, 41–76.

Smith-Burke, M. T. (2001). Reading Recovery: A systemic approach to early intervention. In L. Morrow & D. Woo (Eds.), *Tutoring programs for struggling readers: The America Reads Challenge* (pp. 216–236). New York: Guilford.

Wasik, B. (1998). Volunteer tutoring programs in reading: A review. *Reading Research Quarterly, 33*, 266–292.

Wasik, B., & Slavin, R. (1990). *Preventing early reading failure with one-to-one tutoring: A best evidence synthesis.* Paper presented at the annual convention of the American Educational Research Association, Boston.

Wasik, B., & Slavin, R. (1993). Preventing early reading failure with one-to-one tutoring: A review of five programs. *Reading Research Quarterly, 28*, 178–200.

5

Success for All: An Approach to Schoolwide Reading Reform

Robert E. Slavin

The teaching strategies discussed in the preceding chapters have evidence of effectiveness and have been used in many schools to improve the reading performance of elementary children.* Any school can use any one of these strategies by itself to enhance what its teachers are doing. However, some schools serving large numbers of at-risk readers may want and need to do much more. How could such schools undertake a schoolwide, comprehensive reform process based on well-validated strategies?

Success for All (Slavin & Madden, 2001) is one answer to this question. Success for All is a school reform model that introduces research-based practices throughout a school's essential functions: curriculum, instruction, professional development, school organization, leadership, tutoring, family support, and other elements. A given school could adopt Success for All practices singly, or in combination, to help improve its reading instruction. However, what is unique about Success for All is that it combines research-based practices into a coherent program whose purpose is to help every child learn to read. In this chapter, I describe Success for All as a program, but my intent is also to give an example of what any elementary school might do to build a schoolwide approach to literacy reform.

Success for All Components

While Success for All ultimately incorporates reform in most of the elementary school curriculum and instruction, the heart of the instructional program is reading. The reason for this is obvious; in the early grades, success in school is virtually

*This chapter is adapted from Slavin & Madden, 2001.

synonymous with success in reading. Very few primary-grade students are retained or assigned to special education solely on the basis of deficits in math performance, for example. A child who can read is not guaranteed to be a success in elementary school, but a child who cannot is guaranteed to be a failure. The basic components of Success for All are described below.

Grouping

Homeroom classes in Success for All are fully heterogeneous. However, in order to have enough instructional time to be able to teach reading in many different ways, students are regrouped for reading across grade lines according to reading level, so that all reading classes contain just one level. For example, a reading class working at an early second-grade level might contain first, second, and third graders all reading at the same level. During reading time (ninety minutes per day), additional teachers are available to teach reading because certified tutors (and, in some schools, media specialists, and physical education, special education, or ESL teachers) teach a reading class. This means that reading classes are smaller than homeroom classes. Based on regular curriculum-based assessments given every eight weeks, reading group assignments are constantly reexamined (see below). Students capable of working in a higher-performing group are accelerated, while those who are not performing adequately are given tutoring, family support services, modifications in curriculum or instruction, or other services to help them keep up. Only very rarely would a child repeat a given segment of instruction.

There are many reasons for cross-class and cross-grade grouping for reading in Success for All. First, having all students at one reading level avoids any need for the use of reading groups *within* the class. The problem with reading groups is that, when the teacher is working with one group, the other groups are often at their desks doing seatwork or other independent tasks of little instructional value. To have a full ninety minutes of active, productive instruction, having only one reading group is essential. Research on cross-grade grouping for reading, often called the Joplin Plan, has shown that this method increases student achievement (Slavin, 1987).

In addition, use of cross-class and cross-grade grouping allows the use of tutors and other certified staff as reading teachers. This has many benefits. First, it reduces class size for reading, which has important benefits for achievement in the early grades (Slavin, 1994). Perhaps of equal importance, it gives tutors and other supplementary teachers experience in teaching the reading program so that they know exactly what their students are experiencing. When a student is struggling with Lesson 17, the tutor knows what Lesson 17 is because he or she has taught it.

Eight-Week Assessments

A critical feature of reading instruction in Success for All at all grade levels is assessment of student progress every eight weeks. These assessments are closely linked to the curriculum. In the early grades they may include some written and some oral assessments; in the later grades they use written assessments keyed to novels (if the school uses novels) or may use "magazine tests" or other assessments provided with basal series. Eight-week assessments usually include assessments of skills above students' current level of performance to facilitate decisions to accelerate students to a higher reading group.

Eight-week assessments are used for three essential purposes. One is to change students' reading groupings, to identify students capable of being accelerated. A second is to decide which students are in the greatest need for tutoring and which no longer need tutoring. Finally, the eight-week assessments provide an internal check on the progress of every child. They can indicate to school staff that a given student is not making adequate progress and lead them to try other strategies.

The eight-week assessments are given and scored by reading teachers but are collated and interpreted by the school-based facilitator, who uses them to review the progress of all children and to suggest changes in grouping, tutoring assignments, or other approaches to the reading teachers.

Reading Tutors

One of the most important elements of the Success for All model is the use of tutors to promote students' success in reading. One-to-one tutoring is the most effective form of instruction known (see Wasik & Slavin, 1993). The tutors are certified teachers with experience teaching Title I, special education, and/or primary reading. Often, well-qualified paraprofessionals also tutor children with less severe reading problems. In this case, a certified tutor monitors their work and assists with the diagnostic assessment and intervention strategies. Tutors work one-on-one with students who are having difficulties keeping up with their reading groups. The tutoring occurs in twenty-minute sessions during times other than reading or math periods.

In general, tutors support students' success in the regular reading curriculum rather than teaching different objectives. For example, the tutor will work with a student on the same story and concepts being read and taught in the regular reading class. However, tutors seek to identify learning problems and use different strategies to teach the same skills. They also teach metacognitive skills beyond those taught in the classroom program. Schools may have as many as six or more teachers serving as tutors depending on school size, need for tutoring, and other factors.

During daily ninety-minute reading periods, certified tutors serve as additional reading teachers to reduce class size for reading. Reading teachers and tutors use brief forms to communicate about students' specific problems and needs and meet at regular times to coordinate their approaches with individual children.

Initial decisions about reading group placement and the need for tutoring are based on informal reading inventories that the tutors give to each child. Subsequent reading group placements and tutoring assignments are made using the curriculum-based assessments described previously. First graders receive priority for tutoring, on the assumption that the primary function of the tutors is to help all students be successful in reading the first time, before they fail and become remedial readers.

Preschool and Kindergarten

Most Success for All schools provide a half-day preschool and/or a full-day kindergarten for eligible students. The preschool and kindergarten programs focus on providing a balanced and developmentally appropriate learning experience for young children. The curriculum emphasizes the development and use of language. It provides a balance of academic readiness and nonacademic music, art, and movement activities in a series of thematic units. Readiness activities include use of oral language development activities and Story Telling and Retelling (STaR) in which students retell stories read by the teachers. Prereading activities begin during the second semester of kindergarten.

Family Support Team

Parents are an essential part of the formula for success in Success for All. A Family Support Team works in each school, serving to make families feel comfortable in the school and become active supporters of their child's education as well as providing specific services. The Family Support Team consists of the school's parent liaison, vice principal (if any), counselor (if any), program facilitator, and any other appropriate staff already present in the school or added to the school staff.

The Family Support Team first works toward good relations with parents and to increase their involvement in the school. Family Support Team members may complete "welcome" visits for new families. They organize many attractive programs in the school, such as parenting skills workshops. Many schools use a program called "Raising Readers" in which parents are given strategies to use in reading with their own children.

The Family Support Team also intervenes to solve problems. For example, they may contact parents whose children are frequently absent to see what resources can be provided to assist the family in getting their child to school. Family support staff, teachers, and parents work together to solve school behavior problems. Also, family support staff are called on to provide assistance when students seem to be working at less than their full potential because of problems at home. Families of students who are not receiving adequate sleep or nutrition, need glasses, are not attending school regularly, or are exhibiting serious behavior problems may receive family support assistance.

The Family Support Team is strongly integrated into the academic program of the school. It receives referrals from teachers and tutors regarding children who are not making adequate academic progress, and thereby constitutes an additional stage of intervention for students in need above and beyond that provided by the classroom teacher or tutor. The Family Support Team also encourages and trains the parents to fulfill numerous volunteer roles within the school, ranging from providing a listening ear to emerging readers to helping in the school cafeteria.

Program Facilitator

A program facilitator works at each school to oversee (with the principal) the operation of the Success for All model. The facilitator helps plan the Success for All program, helps the principal with scheduling, and visits classes and tutoring sessions frequently to help teachers and tutors with individual problems. He or she works directly with the teachers on implementation of the curriculum, classroom management, and other issues, helps teachers and tutors deal with any behavior problems or other special problems, and coordinates the activities of the Family Support Team with those of the instructional staff.

Reading Approaches

The philosophy that guides the development of the reading curriculum in Success for All emphasizes the need for reading instruction to work for all students. We recognize that different children learn to read in different ways, so our approach emphasizes teaching reading many different ways at the same time. For example, each beginning reading lesson has students reading silently and aloud, singing, tracing letters with their fingers, writing, making visual and auditory discriminations, discussing stories, making predictions, using context clues, and engaging in many other activities. Teaching the same concepts and skills in many different ways both provides reinforcement and allows the curriculum to utilize the learning strengths of every child.

The Success for All reading approach is divided into two programs. Reading Roots (Madden, 1999) is usually introduced either in the middle of kindergarten or the beginning of first grade, depending on the district's goals for kindergarten. Reading Roots continues through what would usually be thought of as the first reader (1-2 level), and is usually completed by the end of first grade, although a small number of students may not finish Reading Roots until second grade. Reading Roots replaces the usual basals and workbooks with a completely different set of materials. Bilingual schools choosing to teach beginning reading to their Spanish speaking students in Spanish use Lee Conmigo, which uses the same instructional strategies and processes as Reading Roots but is built around stories and materials in Spanish.

Starting at the second-grade level, students go on to what we call Reading Wings, which continues through the fifth or sixth grade. Reading Wings (Madden, Slavin, Farnish, Livingston, & Calderón, 1999) uses the district's usual basals, anthologies, and/or novels, but replaces workbooks and other supplementary materials with a student-centered cooperative learning process that focuses on developing comprehension skills. Reading Wings involves students in many kinds of active interaction with reading, discussion, and writing. The Reading Wings process, when used with Spanish novels or basals, is called Alas Para Leer.

Reading Roots (First Grade)

There is both magic and method in learning to read. Students come to school knowing that learning to read will be their most important task, and that it will be an exciting step in growing up. Taught with effective methods, every child can experience the magic of reading and become a confident, joyful, and strategic reader by the end of first grade.

The Reading Roots program (Madden, 1999) used in Success for All is based on research that points to the need to have students learn to read in meaningful contexts and, at the same time, to have a systematic presentation of word attack skills (see Adams, 1990). Three basic components—reading of children's literature by the teacher, "shared story" beginning reading lessons, and systematic word recognition instruction—combine to address the learning needs of first graders in a variety of ways.

Building Listening Comprehension. A major principle of Reading Roots is that students need to learn comprehension strategies at a level *above* their current independent reading level. What this means is that the teacher reads children's literature to students and engages students in discussions, retelling of the stories, and writing. The idea is to build reading comprehension skill with material more difficult than that which students could read on their own, because in the early grades the material children can read independently does not challenge their far more advanced comprehension skills. This process begins in preschool and kindergarten with a program called Story Telling and Retelling (STaR). STaR continues through first grade. At that point, students begin a Listening Comprehension program in which teachers continue to read to them and teach them to identify characters, settings, problems, and problem solutions in narratives; to visualize descriptive elements of stories; to identify sequences of events; to predict story outcomes; to identify topics and main ideas in expository selections, and so on.

Building Reading Strategies. Before entering Reading Roots, or early in the program, we expect that students have developed basic concepts about print: that we read from left to right; that spoken words match to printed words in text; and that spoken words are made up of sounds that match to letters. These concepts continue to be developed with storytelling (STaR) and are reinforced as students begin to take on the task of reading for themselves in Reading Roots lessons. More specific knowledge involving hearing sounds within words, letter–sound relationships, and blending letter sounds into words are developed in Reading Roots lessons so that students can use phonics cues to help them read.

Reading Roots lessons are structured and fast-paced, involving activities that enable students to learn the new sounds and words introduced in the story thoroughly and quickly. In addition, the lessons develop general strategies for facilitating both word recognition and text comprehension so that students become independent, thinking readers who experience the joy of reading. The activities in Reading Roots incorporate several components:

Shared Stories.   Shared Stories allow students to read complex, engaging, and interesting stories when they only know a few letter sounds. Each page in a Shared Story has both a teacher section and a student section. Beginning in Lesson 4, the students' portions of the shared stories use a phonetically regular vocabulary, so that the skills students are learning will work in cracking the reading code. The student sections use only the letter sounds and words students have learned, plus a few key sight words and "readles," (words represented by pictures). The sections read by the teacher provide a context for the story and include predictive questions that are answered in the student sections. In the earliest stories, the teacher text adds a great deal to the meaning of the stories, but over time the student sections increase while the teacher sections diminish. This "scaffolding" method allows children to read meaningful and worthwhile stories from the first weeks of their beginning reading instruction. As they learn systematic strategies for finding the meaning of words, sentences, and stories, students take increasing responsibility for their reading. Soon they are able to unlock the reading code and join the wacky world of Matt and his dog, Sad Sam, the world's most phonetically regular hound dog; Miss Sid, the pesky parrot; Nan and her cat, Pit-Pat; and many other engaging characters. Later, students meet Lana and her huge dog, Fang; Paco and his mischievous friend, Bob; finally, during the last quarter of the shared story sequence, they experience fairy tales and stories from many cultures. At this level (Level 4), teacher text is no longer used, and the student text presents a challenging reading experience that is designed to help students make the transition between the carefully sequenced Reading Roots lessons and the novels or basals that students will use in Reading Wings. A sample page from a shared story presented in the early part of the sequence and another presented in the latter part are shown in Figures 5.1 and 5.2.

Cooperative Learning.   Working cooperatively with other students provides children with an opportunity to discuss the concepts and skills they are learning with someone very close to their own level of understanding. In Reading Roots, students confer with their partners as they think of words that begin with a certain sound, as they predict the next event in a story, and as they orally read and reread new and familiar stories. These cooperative learning activities provide opportunities for students to explain their understanding to someone else, thus requiring them to organize their own thoughts. Simple peer practice routines are used throughout the lessons as a means of reinforcing and building mastery of basic reading skills. These activities increase the amount of time that each student can be actively engaged with text rather than passively listening as other students read. Opportunities for partner discussion of the story and of story-related writing increase the active thinking time for students.

Scott and Tanya practice kicking her ball during recess. Lana joins them. What will happen to the ball?

Scott rolls the ball.
BAM!
Tanya kicks it.
She *runs* fast.
Lana says, "The ball is off the field!"

FIGURE 5.1 *Page from a shared story.*

Metacognitive Strategies Instruction. Metacognitive skills are emphasized throughout Reading Roots to help students think about the process of reading, to predict what is going to happen in a story, to assess their own comprehension, and to know how to find meaning when they experience difficulties. Four main strategies used to enhance text comprehension are taught and practiced in the context of the Shared Stories: (1) understanding the purposes for reading; (2) previewing to prepare for reading; (3) monitoring for meaning to insure that the text is understood; and (4) summarizing or retelling the main ideas or events of a story.

Phoneme Awareness and Sound Blending. The activities in these lessons are designed to build phoneme awareness (hearing the separate sounds in words) and sound-blending skills in a developmental sequence, so that students will be able to use sound blending as a strategy to aid them in word recognition. With systematic teaching, students become adept at using sound-blending strategies in addition to memory, context, and pictures to unlock the meaning of words and stories. Sound-blending instruction gives a boost to the many students whose visual memory skills

Lots of other things were invented in China. Paper-cut pictures were invented there. Some paper-cut pictures are red for good luck.

Last year, May Woo made a paper-cut picture for the New Year feast. She cut a long dragon out of red paper. Then she looped it in the room where all the farm families celebrated.

FIGURE 5.2   *Page from a shared story—late Grade 1.*

are not strong, a group that often includes students who would fail in reading without this kind of systematic approach to unlocking the reading code.

Writing.   Students are encouraged to write to reinforce their learning and to express their response to stories. Writing activities may vary from completing simple letter and word writing activities that reinforce letter shapes and sounds, to answering specific questions about a story, writing personal experiences similar to those in a story, sharing feelings about characters, and summarizing story events. Sound-based spelling is explicitly taught, and teachers are encouraged to respond to the meaning of the ideas students express rather than to errors in spelling or punctuation. Peers assist one another in the writing process as they share their plans and drafts with one another, revise based on peers' suggestions, and celebrate each others' writing.

Lee Conmigo, the Spanish version of Reading Roots, uses the same lesson structure and instructional processes. The only difference is that the Lee Conmigo reading materials are adapted to follow a sequence of letter presentation appropriate to the Spanish language.

Reading Wings

Reading Wings (Madden, Slavin, Farnish, Livingston, & Calderón, 1999) is the reading approach used in Success for All from the second-grade level to the end of elementary school. It is an adaptation of Cooperative Integrated Reading and Composition (CIRC), a cooperative learning program that encompasses both reading and writing/language arts. Studies of CIRC have shown it to be effective in increasing students' reading, writing, and language achievement (Stevens, Madden, Slavin, & Farnish, 1987).

The curricular focus of Reading Wings is primarily on building comprehension and thinking skills, fluency, and pleasure in reading. Reading Wings assumes that students coming out of Reading Roots have solid word-attack skills, but need to build on this foundation to understand and enjoy increasingly complex material.

As in Reading Roots, students in Reading Wings are regrouped for reading across grade lines, so a 3-1 reading class could be composed of second, third, and fourth graders. In addition, students are assigned to four- or five-member learning teams that are heterogeneous in performance level, sex, and age. These teams choose team names and sit together at most times. The teams have a responsibility to see that all team members are learning the material being taught in class. Each week, students take a set of quizzes. These contribute to a team score, and the teams can earn certificates and other recognition based on the team's average quiz scores. Students also contribute points to their teams by completing book reports and writing assignments, and by returning completed parent forms indicating that they have been reading at home each evening (see below). Figure 5.3 shows a sample score sheet.

Story-Related Activities. Students use their regular basal readers, novels, anthologies, or whatever materials are available in the school. Guides, called Treasure Hunts, have been developed to accompany a large number of current basals and novels, including Spanish basals and novels.

Stories are introduced and discussed by the teacher. During these structured lessons, teachers elicit and provide background knowledge, set a purpose for reading, introduce new and review old vocabulary, discuss the story after students have read it, and so on. Story discussions are structured to emphasize such skills as making and supporting predictions about the story and understanding major structural components of the story (e.g., problem and solution in a narrative).

After stories are introduced, students are given a series of activities to do in their teams when they are not working with the teacher in a reading group. The sequence of activities is as follows:

1. *Partner Reading.* Students read the story silently first, and then take turns reading the story aloud with their partners, alternating readers after each paragraph. As his or her partner reads, the listener follows along and corrects any errors the reader makes.

Team: _____   **Story Title:** _____   **Week of:** _____

Team Members	Words Out Loud Test	Story Test	Meaningful Sentence Assess.	Reading Comp. Test	Adventures in Writing	Team Work Points	Book Response 1	Book Response 2	Read & Respond Form*	Total	Average

*Do not count this column of bonus points when determining the number of columns to divide by.

Team Total

Team Score

Team Cooperation Points

Day 1	Day 2	Day 3	Day 4	Day 5

FIGURE 5.3 *Team Score Sheet*

2. *Story Structure and Story-Related Writing.* Students are given questions related to each narrative story emphasizing the story structure (characters, setting, problem, and problem solution). Halfway through the story, they are instructed to stop reading and to identify the characters, the setting, and the problem in the story, and to predict how the problem will be resolved. At the end of the story, students respond to the story as a whole and write a few paragraphs on a topic related to the story (for example, they might be asked to write a different ending to the story).

3. *Words Out Loud.* Students are given a list of new or difficult words used in the story that they must be able to read correctly in any order. These words are presented by the teacher in the reading group, and then students practice their lists with their partners or other teammates until they can read them smoothly.

4. *Word Meaning.* Students are given a list of story words that are new in their speaking vocabularies and asked to write a sentence for each that shows the meaning of the word (i.e., "An *octopus* grabbed the swimmer with its eight long legs," not "I have an *octopus*"). At higher grade levels, students are asked to look some of the words up in the dictionary and paraphrase the definition.

5. *Story Retell.* After reading the story and discussing it in their reading groups, students summarize the main points of the story to their partners. The partners have a list of essential story elements that they use to check the completeness of the story summaries.

6. *Spelling.* Students pretest one another on a list of spelling words each week, and then work over the course of the week to help one another master the list. Students use a "disappearing list" strategy in which they make new lists of missed words after each assessment until the list disappears and they can go back to the full list, repeating the process as many times as necessary.

Partner Checking. After students complete each of the activities just described, their partners initial a student assignment record form indicating that they have completed and/or achieved criterion on that task. Students are given daily expectations as to the number of activities to be completed, but they can go at their own rate and complete the activities earlier if they wish, creating additional time for independent reading (see below).

Tests. At the end of three class periods, students are given a comprehension test on the story, are asked to write meaningful sentences for certain vocabulary words, and are asked to read the word list aloud to the teacher. Students are not permitted to help one another on these tests. The test scores and evaluations of the story-related writing are major components of students' weekly team scores.

The energy and excitement in Reading Wings comes from the teamwork. Students become very involved with their team members and want to ensure that they are all succeeding. As students become more skilled, the discussion between partners and among team members becomes rich and challenging. Students no longer simply look for the right answer; they demand reasons and evidence to support answers. Books and stories come alive for students as they engage in meaningful discussion with their peers about their responses to their reading. Their enjoyment of reading grows as their increasing skill and fluency allow them to read more and more complex material. (Note: The Reading Wings process for students reading in Spanish, called Alas Para Leer, is the same as for students reading in English.)

Listening Comprehension.   Listening Comprehension provides an additional opportunity to stretch students' ability to understand more and more complex language in a variety of texts. Each day, the teacher reads to students from a novel, anthology, newspaper, magazine, or other source of text at students' interest level but above their current reading level. The teacher then uses the reading as an opportunity to present a lesson focusing on comprehension skills, such as visualization of story characters and settings; identification of problems and attempts to solve problems; story mapping; or sequence of events in narratives. More advanced lessons deal with aspects of authors' craft such as similes and metaphors, the creation of mood, character development, and utilizing information from expository texts.

Direct Instruction in Reading Comprehension.   Students receive direct instruction from the teacher in reading comprehension skills such as identifying main ideas, drawing conclusions, and comparing and contrasting ideas. A special curriculum was designed for this purpose. After each lesson, students work on reading comprehension worksheets and/or games as a whole team, first gaining consensus on one set of worksheet items, then practicing independently, assessing one another's work, and discussing any remaining problems on a second set of items.

Independent Reading.   Every evening, students are asked to read a tradebook of their choice for at least twenty minutes. In most schools, classroom libraries of paperback books are established for this purpose. Parents initial forms indicating that students have read for the required time, and students contribute points to their teams if they submit a completed form each week. In a twice-weekly "book club," students discuss the books they have been reading and present more formal book reports, trying to entice others to take home the same book. "Book reports" can take many forms, from the completion of a brief summary form to an oral summary, advertisement, puppet show, or whatever other form the reader and teacher wish to use. Independent reading and book reports replace all other homework in reading and language arts. If students complete their story-related activities or other activities early, they may also read their independent reading books in class.

Writing and Language Arts

Writing and language arts are critical elements of Success for All; in fact, writing is viewed as the opposite side of the reading coin. In prekindergarten, kindergarten, and first grade, emergent literacy strategies such as journal writing, shared writing, and sound-based spelling are used to build students' interest in expressing their ideas in writing. In Reading Roots and Lee Conmigo, students regularly write in response to the story or to give their answers to questions about the story. In Reading Wings, students exercise their writing skills in response to Treasure Hunt questions and in creative story-related writing activities.

All of these activities use writing to support the learning of reading while providing opportunities to write. However, students also need specific instruction in how to improve their writing. A formal writing/language arts instructional program is usually introduced in Success for All when most teachers are comfortable with the reading program. In practice, this usually means that the writing/language arts program is introduced in the spring of the first implementation year or in the fall of the second year.

Writing/language arts instruction in Success for All is usually provided to students in their heterogeneous homerooms, not in their reading groups. The basic philosophy behind the writing/language arts programs is that writing should be given the main emphasis and that language arts, especially mechanics and usage, should be taught in the context of writing, not as a separate topic.

There are two levels in the Success for All writing and language arts approach. Both are based on writing process theory (Calkins, 1983; Graves, 1983), which emphasizes writing for a real audience, writing for revision, and gradually building spelling and mechanics competence in the context of writing. Writing from the Heart, used in grades 1 and 2, uses an informal version of writing process, while CIRC Writing Wings, used in grades 3–6, uses a more formal writing process model with regular four-member peer-response groups and students working compositions through from plan to draft to revision to editing to publication.

Writing from the Heart (Primary)

A young child thinks of writing as an extension of oral communication. Most, given the undivided attention of an audience, will talk endlessly about their experiences. Young authors rarely have a problem of too little to say; their problem is overcoming the barriers they perceive to putting their ideas down on paper.

The goal of Writing from the Heart (Madden, Wasik, & Petza, 1989), the writing/language arts program used in grades 1 and 2 in Success for All, is to tap students' innate desire, energy, and enthusiasm for communication and to move them to the next step of sharing their ideas with others through writing. When writing is seen as mastery of spelling and mechanics, it is a formidable task. Young students will ultimately need to master these skills, but first they need to develop pleasure and fluency in putting their thoughts on paper. Most importantly, students need to see writing as personal expression, not an ordinary school task. They must put their hearts into their writing, not just their minds.

Writing from the Heart uses a writing process model, which means that students write for a real audience and learn to revise their writing until it is ready for "publication." Students do not work in formal writing teams (that will come in third grade), but they do work informally with partners while they are writing. Writing from the Heart relies on several sequenced elements.

1. *Modeling and Motivating Writing.* At the beginning of each lesson, the teacher provides a model or motivator for writing. For example, the teacher may read a story that is like what students will be writing, or may ask them to describe experiences that relate to a particular kind of writing. The teacher may introduce formats to help students plan their writing. For example, in writing about "myself," students are given a set of questions to answer about themselves which they then use to put into a story.

2. *Writing a "Sloppy Copy."* Students are encouraged to write a "sloppy copy," a first draft of their composition. They are taught to use "sound spelling" (invented spelling) if they cannot spell a word. For example, DINASR is one way a student might write *dinosaur.*

3. *Partner Sharing.* At several points in the writing process students share their writing with partners and receive feedback and ideas from them.

4. *Revision.* Students learn to revise their compositions using feedback from partners and from the teacher. Specific revision skills are taught and modeled in the lessons. Students learn to add the information necessary to help their audience follow and enjoy their story.

5. *Editing.* In preparation for publication, the teacher helps each child prepare a perfect draft of his or her composition, complete with pictures. This is when DINASR becomes *dinosaur.*

6. *Publication.* Final drafts of students' writings are "published" in a class book, read to the class, and recognized in as many ways as the teacher can think of.

7. *Sharing and celebration.* At many points in the writing process students have opportunities to share their writing with the class. The teacher sets up a special "author's chair" from which the "authors" present their latest works. Authors are taught to ask three questions of their audience:
- What did you hear? Can you tell me about my story?
- What did you like about my story?
- What else would you like to know about my story?

The teacher models use of the author's chair by presenting his or her own writing and models answers to the author's questions.

Writing from the Heart prepares students for the Writing Wings program starting in grade 3 by convincing them that they are authors and have something to say, by teaching them that writing is a process of thinking, drafting, revising, and polishing ideas, and by letting them know that writing is fun. They are then ready to learn more about the craft of writing with more formal instruction in tricks of the trade, style, mechanics, and usage.

Writing Wings (Upper Elementary)

The writing/language arts program used in the upper elementary grades is one developed earlier as part of Cooperative Integrated Reading and Composition (CIRC) for grades 3 and up (Madden, Farnish, Slavin, Stevens, & Sauer, 1999). In this program, students are assigned to four- or five-member heterogeneous writing teams. Writing Wings has two major instructional formats. About three days each week are used for writing process activities, and two for language arts instruction.

Writing Process Activities

Writing Concept Lessons. Each writing process day begins with a brief lesson on a writing concept. For example, the first lesson is on "mind movies," visualization of events in a narrative to see where additional detail or description is needed. Other lessons include organizing imaginative narratives, using observation to add life to descriptions, writing personal narratives, mysteries, persuasive arguments, explanatory writing, and so on. The writing concept lessons are meant to spark ideas and help students expand on their writing and evaluate their own and others' compositions.

Writing Process. Most of the writing/language arts period is spent with students writing their own compositions while the teacher circulates among the teams and conferences with individual students. Students draft many compositions and then choose a smaller number they would like to carry all the way through the five steps to publication.

   1. *Prewriting.* Students discuss with their teammates a topic they would like to address and an audience for their writing. They then draft a plan, using a "skeleton planning form," an "idea net," or other forms to organize their thinking.

   2. *Drafting.* After the student prepares a plan in consultation with teammates, he or she writes a first draft, focusing on getting ideas on paper rather than spelling and mechanics (they will come later).

   3. *Team Response and Revision.* Students read their drafts to their teammates. The teammates are taught to rephrase the main idea of the story in their own words, to mention two things they liked about the story, and to note two things they'd like to hear more about. The teacher may also conference with students at the revision stage to applaud their ideas and suggest additions and changes. Specific revision guides for specific categories of writing assist students in responding usefully to their teammates' writing. For instance, as students learn to enrich their narratives with rich description, they use a team-response guide that asks them to tell the author (their teammate) their favorite descriptive words. As they look at the writing of their teammates, they learn to look for those features in their own writing. Students make revisions based on their teammates' responses.

4. *Editing.* Once the author is satisfied with the content of the writing, he or she is ready to correct the mechanics, usage, and spelling. Students work with a partner to go through an editing checklist. The checklist starts with a small number of goals (e.g., correct capitalization and end punctuation), but then adds goals as students complete language arts lessons. For example, after a lesson on subject–verb agreement or run-on sentences, these skills may be added to the checklist. The author first checks the composition against the checklist, then a teammate does so, and finally the teacher checks it.

5. *Publication.* Publication involves the creation of the final draft and celebration of the author's writing. Students carefully rewrite their work incorporating all final corrections made by the teacher. They then present their compositions to the class from a fancy "author's chair," and may then contribute their writing to a team book or a team section of a class book. These books are proudly displayed in the classroom or in the school library. In addition, students may be asked to read their compositions to other classes or to otherwise celebrate and disseminate their masterpieces!

Revision and Editing Skills Lessons. About two days each week the teacher teaches structured lessons on language mechanics skills. These are presented as skills for revision and editing because their purpose is to directly support students' writing. The teacher determines the order of lessons according to problems students are experiencing and skills they will need for upcoming writing. For example, the teacher may notice that many students are having problems within complete sentences, or he/she may anticipate that because students are about to write dialogue they need to learn how to use quotation marks.

Students work in their four-member writing teams to help one another master the skills taught by the teacher. The students work on examples, compare answers with each other, resolve discrepancies, explain ideas to each other, and so on. Ultimately students are quizzed on the skill, and the teams can earn certificates or other recognition based on the average performance of all team members. As noted earlier, immediately after a revision and editing skills lesson the new skill is added to the editing checklist, so language arts skills are immediately put into practice in students' writing.

Research on Success for All

From the very beginning, there has been a strong focus in Success for All on research and evaluation. Evaluations have compared Success for All schools to matched comparison schools on individually administered measures of reading performance, starting with cohorts in kindergarten or in first grade and continuing to follow these students as long as possible. Vagaries of funding and other local problems have ended some evaluations prematurely, but most evaluations have been able to follow Success for All schools for many years. There are seven years of continuous data from the six original schools in Baltimore and Philadelphia, and varying numbers of years of data from seven other districts, a total of twenty-three schools (and their matched control schools).

In all cases, reading tests were administered by testers who were unaffiliated with the project. Every attempt was made to keep testers unaware of whether a school was a Success for All or a control school. Testers were trained to a high degree of reliability and then observed on a sampling basis to be sure they were administering the tests properly.

Each of the evaluations using individual reading measures follows children who began Success for All (SFA) in first grade or earlier, in comparison to children who had attended the control school over the same period. In other studies, gains in SFA schools' scores on state accountability measures were compared to those in the state or district as a whole. For more details on methods and findings, see Slavin & Madden (2001).

The results of the multi-site replicated experiment evaluating Success for All are summarized in Figure 5.4, which incorporates data from about 6000 students. Statistically significant (p=.05 or better) positive effects of Success for All (compared

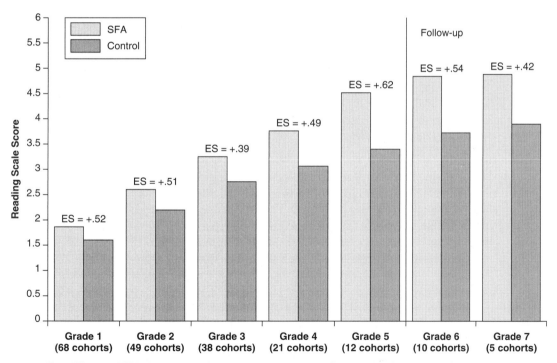

Note: Effect size (ES) is the proportion of a standard deviation by which Success for All Students exceeded controls. Includes approximately 6000 children in Success for All or control schools since first grade.

FIGURE 5.4 *Comparison of Success for All and Control Schools in Mean Reading Grade Equivalents and Effect Sizes, 1988–1999*

to controls) were found on every measure at every grade level, 1–5. In addition, positive effects maintained into grades six and seven, when children had gone on to middle school. Effect sizes for students in the lowest 25 percent of their grades were particularly positive, as were effects for limited English proficient students (see Slavin & Madden, 1999).

Large-scale studies of the effects of Success for All on state accountability tests have also found strong positive impacts (Hurley, Chamberlain, Slavin, & Madden, 2001; Sanders, Wright, & Ross, 2000). Two studies found a significant relationship between the degree of program implementation and student outcomes (Nunnery et al., 1996; Ross, Smith, & Casey, 1997). In addition, several studies have found substantial reductions in special education placements in Success for All schools, and improvements in the achievement of children categorized as learning disabled (Slavin, 1996; Smith, Ross, & Casey, 1994).

Conclusion

The results of evaluations of Success for All schools in many districts throughout the United States clearly show that the program increases student reading perform-ance. In almost every evaluation, Success for All students learned significantly more than matched control students. Significant effects were not seen on every measure at every grade level, but the consistent direction and magnitude of the effects show unequivocal benefits for Success for All students. Evidence showed particularly large impacts on the achievement of limited English proficient students in both bilingual and ESL programs, and on both reducing special education referrals and improving the achievement of students who have been assigned to special education.

The demonstration that an effective program can be replicated and can be effective in its replication sites removes one more excuse for the continuing low achievement of disadvantaged children.

Clearly, preventing children from experiencing reading problems in the first place makes far more sense than allowing them to fall behind and only then providing remedial or special education services. Success for All provides one demonstration that prevention and early intervention can make a substantial dif-ference in the school success of at-risk children.

References

Adams, M. J. (1990). *Beginning to read: Thinking and learning about print.* Cambridge, MA: MIT Press.

Calkins, L. M. (1983). *Lessons from a child: On the teaching and learning of writings.* Exeter, NH: Heinemann.

Graves, D. (1983). *Writing: Teachers and children at work.* Exeter, NH: Heinemann.

Hurley, E., Chamberlain, A., Slavin, R. E., & Madden, N. A. (2001). Effects of Success for All on TAAS Reading: A Texas statewide evaluation. *Phi Delta Kappan, 82*(10), 750–756.

Madden, N. A. (1999). *Reading Roots teacher's manual.* Baltimore, MD: Success for All Foundation.

Madden, N. A., Calderón, M., and Rice, L. B. (1999). *Lee Conmigo: Teachers' manual.* Baltimore, MD: Success for All Foundation.

Madden, N. A., Farnish, A. M., Slavin, R. E., Stevens, R. J., & Sauer, D. C. (1999). *CIRC Writing: Manual for teachers.* Baltimore, MD: Success for All Foundation.

Madden, N. A., Slavin, R. E., Farnish, A. M., Livingston, M. A., & Calderón, M. (1999). *Reading Wings teacher's manual.* Baltimore, MD: Success for All Foundation.

Madden, N. A., Wasik, B. A., & Petza, R. J. (1989). *Writing from the Heart: A writing process approach for first and second graders.* Baltimore, MD: Success for All Foundation.

Nunnery, J., Slavin, R. E., Ross, S. M., Smith, L. J., Hunter, P., & Stubbs, J. (1996). *An assessment of Success for All program component configuration effects on the reading achievement of at-risk first grade students.* Paper presented at the annual meeting of the American Educational Research Association, New York.

Ross, S. M., Smith, L. J., & Casey, J. P. (1997). Preventing early school failure: Impacts of Success for All on standardized test outcomes, minority group performance, and school effectiveness. *Journal of Education for Students Placed at Risk, 2*(1), 29–53.

Sanders, W. L., Wright, S. P., & Ross, S. M. (2000). *Four-year results for Roots & Wings schools in Memphis.* Memphis, TN: University of Memphis, Center for Research in Educational Policy.

Slavin, R. E. (1987). Ability grouping and student achievement in elementary schools: A best-evidence synthesis. *Review of Educational Research, 57,* 347–350.

Slavin, R. E. (1994). School and classroom organization in beginning reading: Class size, aides, and instructional grouping. In R. E. Slavin, N. L. Karweit, & B. A.Wasik, (Eds.), *Preventing early school failure: Research on effective strategies* (pp. 122–142). Boston: Allyn & Bacon.

Slavin, R. E. (1996). Neverstreaming: Preventing learning disabilities. *Educational Leadership, 53*(5), 4–7.

Slavin, R. E., & Madden, N. A. (1999). Effects of bilingual and English as a second language adaptations of Success for All on the reading achievement of students acquiring English. *Journal of Education for Students Placed at Risk, 4*(4), 393–416.

Slavin, R. E., & Madden, N. A. (Eds.). (2001). *One million children: Success for All.* Thousand Oaks, CA: Corwin.

Slavin, R. E., Madden, N. A., Dolan, L. J., & Wasik, B. A. (1996). *Every child, every school: Success for All.* Newbury Park, CA: Corwin.

Smith, L. J., Ross, S. M., & Casey, J. P. (1994). *Special education analyses for Success for All in four cities.* Memphis: University of Memphis, Center for Research in Educational Policy.

Stevens, R. J., Madden, N. A., Slavin, R. E., & Farnish, A. M. (1987). Cooperative Integrated Reading and Composition: Two field experiments. *Reading Research Quarterly, 22,* 433–454.

Wasik, B. A., & Slavin, R. E. (1993). Preventing early reading failure with one-to-one tutoring: A review of five programs. *Reading Research Quarterly, 28,* 178–200.

Index